Why the First-Year Seminar Matters

Praise for *Why the First-Year Seminar Matters*

"Harrington and Orosz provide a compelling case for leveraging the power of first-year seminars to help students choose and work towards a career path. This is an important read for educators desiring to better understand how a first-year seminar can play a pivotal role in the Guided Pathways movement."—**Dan Friedman**, director, University 101 programs, University of South Carolina

"Christine Harrington and Theresa Orosz offer a well-researched and compelling argument for increasing college completion by modernizing the first-year seminar and leveraging it as a core element of Guided Pathways. A worthy read."—**Michael Collins**, vice president, Jobs for the Future

"Reform efforts in higher education have approached the challenge of improving student success by accretion—piling on stand-alone initiatives and creating 'initiative fatigue' among those responsible for implementing these initiatives. This book demonstrates how colleges can move beyond initiative addition to initiative integration, resulting in student support that is more synergistic (combining separate initiatives—guided pathways and the first-year seminar—to generate a collective, multiplicative impact on student success); sustainable (building on a well-supported, proactively delivered first-year seminar to generate a long-term educational vocational plan that guides students from college entry to college completion); scalable (providing intrusive, or inescapable, support that reaches the entire student body); and holistic (supporting the student as a 'whole person' and addressing both academic and 'nonacademic,' or personal, factors that affect student success). This book is a must-read for any professional interested in helping students discover their passion, find a path to their future, and develop a systematic plan for navigating that path."—**Joseph B. Cuseo**, professor emeritus, psychology, Marymount California University

Why the First-Year Seminar Matters

Helping Students Choose and Stay on a Career Path

Christine Harrington
Theresa Orosz

ROWMAN & LITTLEFIELD
Lanham • Boulder • New York • London

Published by Rowman & Littlefield
An imprint of The Rowman & Littlefield Publishing Group, Inc.
4501 Forbes Boulevard, Suite 200, Lanham, Maryland 20706
www.rowman.com

Unit A, Whitacre Mews, 26-34 Stannary Street, London SE11 4AB

British Library Cataloguing in Publication Information Available

Library of Congress Cataloging-in-Publication Data Available

ISBN 9781475842463 (cloth : alk. paper) | ISBN 9781475842470 (pbk : alk. paper) | ISBN 9781475842487 (ebook)

♾ ™ The paper used in this publication meets the minimum requirements of American National Standard for Information Sciences Permanence of Paper for Printed Library Materials, ANSI/NISO Z39.48-1992.

Printed in the United States of America

To my students for allowing me to be a part of your pathway and my colleagues who pave the way for student success.

—Christine Harrington

To the students whose inspiring stories inform our work and the dedicated professionals who help our students realize their dreams.

—Theresa Orosz

Contents

Foreword

Melinda Mechur Karp, PhD
founder, Phase Two Advisory

As I reflect on my work with community colleges over the past decade, I am continually awed by the sea change in attitudes within the sector. Ten years ago, student services and advising remained siloed, often an afterthought or a set of boutique programs done "over there" in a part of the college disconnected from academic pursuits. "Reform" was still conceived as small programs serving a subset of students, or a series of pilot activities. Student failure was often attributed to the students themselves or their circumstances outside of school, rather than institutional structures and practices.

Not anymore. Today, most community college practitioners (as well as those in four-year institutions) see the inextricable connection between student services and academic success. They recognize the ways that the organization of college can contribute to student failure or—if changed—student success. "Reform" has shifted from programs to broad, institution-wide redesign that reaches all students. These changes are epitomized by the Guided Pathways movement, which argues for change at scale in order to reach all students in and out of the classroom and maximize the likelihood they will earn a credential.

The rapid growth of the guided pathways movement, as well as related reforms such as technology-mediated student services redesign, epitomizes a new outlook within higher education. This new paradigm seeks to reorganize colleges to provide what research and practitioner experience tells us students need—clear pathways to a degree, strong interpersonal relationships, and a sense of connection between educational pursuits and long-term goals.

At their core, current reform efforts posit that by streamlining information and information provision, space will open up for meaningful engagement between students, instructors, and support personnel. If students have a clearly defined path and advisors can identify whether or not they are making progress on that path, even short advising interactions can focus on relationship building and holistic problem solving rather than the minutia of course scheduling and graduation requirements. As my research and that of so many others has shown, such personal and meaningful engagement is at the core of student persistence and learning.

But as Christine and Theresa point out in this book, the Guided Pathways idea only works if students can select a program of study that makes sense for them and their long-term goals. And as I have long argued, asking students to select a program earlier in their college career makes it even more important that they choose "right," because if they change their mind, they are likely to lose even more credits and time when switching majors than they would have before. Moreover, Guided Pathways and advising redesign efforts typically occur in resource-constrained environments. Colleges are unable to hire substantial numbers of new staff but are being asked to provide more in-depth support all the same.

Given that career and program selection are time-consuming, nuanced, and require personalized engagement, how can resource-constrained colleges effectively guide students to select the program of study that is right for them early in their college careers? One strategy I often suggest, and which many colleges have begun to use, is to implement student mandatory success courses to help students enter and plan a program of study. In this book, Christine and Theresa make the case for doing so, showing how student success courses and Guided Pathways reforms connect to one another.

By infusing the preexisting structure of a student success course with Guided Pathways and career development principles, they argue, colleges can (1) help students get on a path that is meaningful to them and connected to a clear academic trajectory; (2) amplify the course's impact; (3) create the economies of scale necessary for guided pathways institutional reform; and (4) set the stage for keeping students on a path and ensuring their learning later on.

As the authors point out, connecting student success courses to Guided Pathways makes intuitive and empirical sense. These courses already exist on campuses, so repurposing them does not require building an entirely new initiative. They already have a robust evidence base indicating their efficacy in improving student persistence; in fact, my own research has found that well-designed student success courses can have positive impact even beyond students' first year (Karp, Raufman, Efthimiou, & Ritze, 2015). And because student success courses enroll many students at a time and can be taught by a combination of administrative and academic faculty, they have the potential to ensure that all students receive in-depth, personalized support on their way to selecting and planning a program of study without large infusions of new funding.

Of course, as with most "solutions" in education, it's easier to imagine the potential of a reform than make it happen on a campus. We can envision a revised student success course that provides students with personalized relationship building, long-term career planning, connections to programs of study, and culminates in every student having a long-term program plan and relationship with an advisor who can support them over the entirety of their academic career. The vision is lovely.

But the reality is thornier. What would the curriculum look like, really? In most instances, some elements of a traditional student success course will need to be shed to make room for in-depth career exploration and planning. How do administrators convince doubters this is a wise choice?

Christine and Theresa give practitioners information, guidelines, and strategies to answer these questions. They provide a detailed overview of Guided Pathways, career development, and student success courses, giving baseline knowledge to readers unfamiliar with any or all of these bodies of work. Then, by giving a deep-dive into backwards course design, they provide a framework for rethinking and repurposing student success courses with guided pathways and career development principles in mind. Thus, this book helps colleges turn enthusiasm for Guided Pathways, institutional redesign, and student services reform into an integrated onboarding approach that enables all students to select and plan their academic pathway without unduly burdening institutional resources.

Christine and Theresa have seen the challenge of guiding students from the perspectives of a student services provider, instructor, institutional administrator, and system administrator. They bring a practice-oriented lens: How can we get this done? They are able to weave in examples from their experience to show how a Guided-Pathways-focused course redesign plays out in practice. They also discuss specific tactics and approaches to a Guided-Pathways-focused course providing practitioners with a toolkit of ideas from which to pull as they engage in their own redesign, including case-making arguments, which are critical to any redesign effort.

It is gratifying to see one's once-provocative research become "common knowledge" in a sector about which she feels passionately—as I have had the privilege of experiencing. It is even more gratifying to see knowledgeable practitioners guide others in implementing research findings so as to ensure that more students are successful in achieving their educational and post-collegiate goals.

REFERENCE

Karp, M. M., Kaufman, J., Efthimiou, C., & Ritze, N. (2015). *Redesigning a student success course for sustained impact: Early outcomes findings* (CCRC Working Paper No. 81). New York, NY: Columbia University, Teachers College, Community College Research Center.

Part I

Making the Case—FYE as an Essential Part of Guided Pathways

Chapter One

Guided Pathways

In recent years, colleges and universities across the nation have mobilized around Guided Pathways to increase student outcomes. The Guided Pathways movement requires colleges and universities to do the following: clearly define programs so students know what they need to do in order to successfully complete degree requirements, help students choose a career pathway, help students stay on their pathway so they can achieve their goals, and ensure that students are learning throughout the process (Bailey, Jaggars, & Jenkins, 2015). This chapter provides an overview of the Guided Pathways movement, emphasizing the importance of helping students choose and stay on a career pathway.

THE GUIDED PATHWAYS MOVEMENT: WHY IT MATTERS

By the first decade of the 21st century, it was evident that higher education in the United States had reached a crossroads. Decreased funding, calls for increased accountability, and lackluster graduation rates had cast colleges and universities in a less than favorable light. The added realization that the United States was no longer the world leader in postsecondary degree attainment prompted a rallying cry. In 2009, the Obama administration called for 20 million additional college graduates by 2020 (Mullin, 2010). That same year, the Lumina Foundation announced "Goal 2025," intended to increase the number of adults with college degrees, certificates, or high-quality postsecondary credentials to 60% by 2025 (Lumina Foundation, 2016).

Because of these high-profile initiatives at the state and federal levels, priorities began shifting from access to success. More emphasis was being placed on student outcomes. Regional accrediting bodies began to review their standards, student success metrics were revisited, and nonprofit organizations such as the Gates Foundation, Complete College America, and the Kresge Foundation made significant investments in efforts to improve student success (Katz, 2012; Lederman, 2015).

Persistence and Completion Rates

Persistence and completion rates have become a priority for colleges and universities in recent years. In other words, the focus has moved from enrolling students to retaining and graduating students. In fall 2015, the full-time retention rate of students at postsecondary institutions was 74.4%, while the part-time retention rate was 44.9%. For the 2009 cohort year, the graduation rate (within 150% of normal time) was 53.8% at four-year postsecondary institutions. For the 2012 cohort year, the graduation rate (within 150% of normal time) was 31.6% at two-year postsecondary institutions (McFarland, Hussar, de Brey, Snyder, Wang, et al., 2017).

The 100% national graduation rates are even more telling. Only 5% of students at two-year institutions graduate within two years. At four-year institutions, the graduation rates are higher but far from ideal. Excluding the highest-level research universities, at all other four-year institutions only 20% of the fall 2008 cohort of full-time students graduated within four years (Complete College America, 2018). As these figures show, there is room for significant improvement, particularly in terms of retention rates for part-time students and graduation rates at both four-year and two-year institutions.

A study that tracked persistence and graduation rates of part-time students found that 34.4% completed bachelor degrees or higher, while only 6.5% of students completed associate degrees (Inside Track, 2015). It is important to note that students who do not attend college full time make up a large proportion of the community-college population. More than half (56.3%) of the students attending community colleges are at least 25 years old, with family responsibilities and a full-time job (Snyder, 2014). Part-time students at both two- and four-year institutions must not be excluded from the national conversation.

Excess/Unnecessary Credits

When students are graduating, they are often graduating with more credits than necessary. According to Complete College America (2018), the national average number of credits an associate degree–seeking student accumulates by the time of graduation is 82, even though most associate degrees only require the completion of 60 credits. This represents 22 credits (or five to seven extra classes) beyond what is needed to earn a two-year degree.

The situation is similar with bachelor's degrees. Students earning baccalaureate degrees accrue an average of 135 credits despite most baccalaureate degrees only requiring the completion of 120 credits (Complete College America, 2018). This represents 15 credits (or three to five extra classes) beyond what is needed to earn a four-year degree.

Students are spending valuable time and money on unnecessary credits. This means that students are walking away from college with higher than necessary levels of debt. The average student loan debt for a student earning a bachelor's degree is approximately $30,000 (Bidwell, 2014). If students took only the number of credits required for graduation as opposed to taking additional credits that were not program requirements, this amount of debt would be lower.

The increased time spent taking classes rather than working is also a financial concern. As Abel and Dietz (2014) note, there are two types of costs associated with college: direct costs and opportunity costs. Direct costs include costs that stem from tuition, fees, books, or other related educational expenses. Opportunity costs are lost opportunities for earned income. Although many students are working while attending college, they are typically earning a pre-degree salary that is typically much lower than a post-degree salary. Thus, by taking additional courses that are not required in programs, students are delaying the benefit of earning post-degree salaries.

The ramifications for students who receive financial aid are significant. Regulatory changes have made it imperative that students receiving financial aid decide upon a career and select an appropriate major early in their academic studies. Financial aid eligibility depends on students making satisfactory academic progress toward their degree. This limits the breadth of courses that students can take to explore diverse areas of interest. Only courses that can be used to fulfill designated electives or degree requirements will be approved for financial aid (Kantrowicz, 2012).

From a financial standpoint, it is therefore critically important that students select a major early in their college career and then follow that program of study closely so as not to waste time or money. This does not preclude a student from changing majors; however, the later this occurs in their college career, the more financially damaging it may be for students. Students no longer have the luxury of "finding themselves" or trying out multiple majors. This is problematic given that few students begin college knowing exactly what they want to pursue.

Most students who enter college directly after high school do not arrive with a clearly defined career plan. Career exploration in high school is limited at best. In a "Dear Colleagues" letter, the asssistant secretaries of the U.S. Departments of Education, Labor, and Health and Human Services noted that while high school counseling does include a college planning component, career planning and exploration are marginally addressed.

The authors cited three key reasons for this problem. First, the unfavorable ratio of school counselors to students results in small numbers of school counselors working with large numbers of students. This limits the time that counselors can meet with students to help them make informed career choices and to monitor their progress. Next, school counselors' multiple roles require them to spend most of their time on academic achievement issues at the expense of career planning and counseling activities. Finally, counselors' access to the latest information on employment trends and requirements varies among school districts. This can limit students' ability to obtain the necessary information for making sound career choices (Dann-Messier, Wu, & Greenburg, 2014).

The results from a multi-year national College and Career Readiness survey of high school students support the secretaries' concerns. The survey found that less than half (approximately 45%) of respondents felt positively about their college and career readiness. Only 45.7% of students reported that their high schools had helped them determine which careers matched their interests and abilities and only 48.7% of students agreed that their high school helped them understand the steps needed to attain their career goals (Youth Truth Student Survey, 2018).

As the findings illustrate, the majority of high school students who arrive on college campuses have been insufficiently prepared to make appropriate decisions regarding career goals and choice of major. Without proper guidance and structure at the onset of college, these students will waste time, money, and energy as they accumulate unnecessary credits in pursuit of a degree that may not match their career aspirations. This lack of guidance can also contribute to students not completing the degree within the timeframes allocated by financial aid regulations.

Financial aid recipients do not have time on their side. Continued eligibility for federal grants and loans requires students to maintain satisfactory academic progress (SAP). This means that students must graduate within the maximum time frame for their degree program. This equates to 150% of the normal time for their degree program or, in other words, six years for a bachelor's degree and three years for an associate's degree. Students who change majors multiple times may find themselves facing a SAP issue and risk losing or exhausting their financial aid (Kantrowitz, 2012).

These financial aid regulation changes impact large numbers of students. During the 2014–2015 academic year, 86% of first-time, full-time students at four-year institutions and 79% of first-time, full-time students at two-year institutions received financial aid (McFarland et al., 2017). Thus, it is critical that colleges and universities assist students with getting on a path as soon as possible. For these reasons, the implementation of Guided Pathways in a student's first semester is critically important to their success.

Until recently, the higher education sector believed that providing students an unlimited choice of courses and degree programs was good practice. What colleges and universities have come to learn is that while some degree of exploration is beneficial, too much choice and a lack of direction is actually a barrier to completion (Bailey et al., 2015). In response, the Guided Pathways movement emerged as a best practice initiative that supports completion. Rather than providing students with endless choices, Guided Pathways focuses the process of course and program selection through the use of embedded support services and a clear road map for students.

DEFINING GUIDED PATHWAYS

The Guided Pathways movement is focused on improving student success outcomes. Guided Pathways is a campus-wide, collaborative effort among academic and student support areas that assists students with making informed decisions that help them realize their academic and career goals in a timely manner. To be successful, campus-wide support and involvement is needed. Guided Pathways is about institutional reform to improve success outcomes for students.

"Start with the end in mind" is the mantra of the Guided Pathways movement (Jenkins, 2014). Guided Pathways looks to the future. It begins by identifying a student's end goal and keeps that goal at the forefront of all academic and student affairs interactions as the student progresses along their educational journey. For two-year colleges, a student's end goal may be degree completion and successful transfer to a four-year institution or degree completion and employment in their field of study. At four-year institutions, a student's end goal may be degree completion and admittance to a graduate program or degree completion and employment in their field of study.

Guided Pathways reform involves comprehensive changes to college practices and culture. There are four primary pillars associated with the Guided Pathways movement:

1. Defining clear academic pathways
2. Helping students choose and enter a pathway
3. Supporting students along the path to help them meet with success
4. Ensuring that meaningful and significant learning takes place along the path (Jenkins & Cho, 2014; Bailey et al., 2015)

New Jersey has further organized these key components into two primary areas: establishing pathways and helping students navigate pathways. According to this approach, establishing pathways includes defining programs and paths and creating meaningful learning experiences. Thus, establishing pathways involves institutions providing clear road maps for students that articulate graduation requirements for each program and then making sure that significant learning happens along this pathway so that students have the knowledge and skills to be successful in their career.

Navigating pathways, on the other hand, involves helping students choose and stay on a path. More specifically, this involves engaging students in meaningful career exploration and decision making and helping students develop or enhance the skills needed to successfully reach their career goal. Toward this end, academic programs and student support services are redesigned or reorganized to create clearly outlined and logical educational pathways that embed intentional student services interventions at key junctures throughout a student's journey (Center for Student Success at the New Jersey Council of County Colleges, n.d.).

Defining Academic Pathways

To create clearly defined pathways, institutions typically start by developing program maps for each major. The maps provide students with a delineated and sequenced list of recommended and required courses. Program maps provide direction for students and reduce the chance of students taking unnecessary credits.

The concept of articulating degree requirements is not a new one. Colleges and universities have always had general education, major, and elective requirements that students had to fulfill in order to attain a degree. However, in many of these cases, the exact courses required within the different categories were not always clearly communicated to students. In fact, it was often the opposite. Students were provided with literally hundreds of options to choose from to fulfill a requirement. Bailey et al. (2015) note that students can find this lack of structure to be confusing and overwhelming.

Johnstone (2015) notes that "the path through general education at most community colleges resembles the menu at the Cheesecake Factory—hundreds of options and never enough time to even read through them before we are asked to order" (p. 7). To best assist students, recommended general education or elective courses can be shared with students via the program map.

Program maps outline the courses a student must complete in order to earn the degree. This includes core courses specific to the major, along with suggested electives and college-wide graduation requirements. Courses are typically arranged in a recommended sequence that takes into consideration prerequisites, corequisites, and fall-only or spring-only offerings. Before Guided Pathways, colleges and universities shared the requirements needed for degree attainment, but sequencing information was not always provided. Students who understand sequencing issues such as prerequisites and corequisites and who develop an academic plan accordingly are more likely to graduate on time.

It is also important for colleges and universities to identify gateway, or milestone courses, on program maps. Gateway courses are essential courses in a major. For example, Anatomy and Physiology might be a gateway course in a health program. Success in a gateway course can be predictive of whether or not a student will achieve success in the program (Jenkins, Lahr, & Fink, 2017a). Drawing student attention to gateway courses can communicate the importance of key coursework.

To best help students focus on the big picture, program maps can also provide students with meaningful career and transfer information. In other words, making career information easily accessible focuses student attention on the long-term career goal and helps students see the connections between program requirements and skills needed in order to be successful in their chosen career path. Career and transfer information is usually linked to program map web pages, providing students with an overview of the major, job outlook prospects, salary data, campus contact information, and other similar information.

As faculty and administrators at colleges map out the program requirements, it is important to consider whether modifications may be needed. For example, colleges and universities may want to add more experiential learning into the curriculum. Some schools, like Cincinnati State Technical and Community College, have incorporated a mandatory cooperative experience into all of their degree programs.

Participation in at least one co-op experience is required to graduate. As part of the experience, students work with co-op coordinators and attend seminar classes where they prepare résumés, learn interviewing skills, and develop learning outcomes related to their co-op placement (Jenkins, Lahr, & Fink, 2017b). While requiring experiential learning may not be feasible at all institutions, it does illustrate the power of Guided Pathways when partnerships are forged between colleges and local employers.

One of the primary concerns raised by faculty and staff about Guided Pathways in general, and with making course recommendations specifically, is that this appears to prohibit student choice. However, restricting choice was not the intent of Guided Pathways. On the contrary, recommendations are meant to guide not restrict students. In other words, if a student is planning to pursue a career in the field of psychology, program maps can indicate which general education electives best support learning in this field.

This does not necessarily mean that the recommended courses are the only courses that students can choose from; colleges and universities can recommend courses while still allowing students the freedom of choice within a larger menu of options. Johnstone (2015) emphasizes that students still have choice under Guided Pathways but notes that students' time is better spent on choosing a program rather than on selecting courses.

Choosing the right program can be a confusing process for students. As a result, colleges began thinking in terms of meta-majors, a term that, early on, quickly became part of the Guided Pathways vernacular. More recently, colleges and universities are using terms such as career clusters or areas of interest in lieu of the term meta-major because this term was not resonating with students. Meta-majors or career clusters are a way to organize programs by major areas of study. Using a meta-major approach makes decision making more manageable for the student who has not yet decided on a career path. Instead of perhaps over a hundred options, first-year students can first choose from approximately 6 to 10 meta-majors or career cluster areas.

Institutions across the country that are actively implementing Guided Pathways have adopted meta-majors in ways that suit their institutions' cultures and organizational structures. For example, schools in Ohio may have their own individual approach to meta-majors, but they all share a focus on careers. Clark State Community College uses 10 career-oriented "program clusters" to group its degrees (Jenkins, Lahr, & Fink, 2017b). The College System of Tennessee worked together to identify nine "academic foci," groups of disciplines that incorporate all the programs of study offered across all 19 community colleges and universities. These nine areas include Applied Technology, Arts, Business, Education, Health Professions, Humanities, Social Sciences, STEM, and General Education for undecided students or those who want an interdisciplinary option (Denley, n.d.).

Whether broad program groups are referred to as meta-majors, areas of interest, focus areas, or another term that fits the characteristics of the institution, their common goal is to assist students who are not yet decided about a career path. This approach helps students choose a broad career field and then through the first-year seminar course, students can explore specific careers within the broader pathway. Clearly defined program maps can then guide students in reaching their goal.

Creating Meaningful Learning Experiences

According to the Center for Student Success at the New Jersey Council of County Colleges (n.d.), creating meaningful learning experiences is the second pillar of Guided Pathways. Ensuring that students are learning the knowledge and skills needed for success in careers is critical. Unfortunately, the reality in higher education is that faculty are typically hired for their discipline expertise; and in many cases, faculty may not have much, if any, training in best pedagogical practices. In university settings, teaching may not be valued as much as research and scholarship and therefore, there may not be much institutional support for improving teaching and learning practices.

Guided Pathways calls for an increased focus on faculty development, assisting instructors with designing effective courses and using teaching strategies grounded in theory and research. Sorcinelli, Berg, Bond, and Watson (2017) note that there is extensive research connecting faculty development to student success outcomes. In other words, investing in professional development leads to higher levels of student achievement. In order to be most effective, professional development needs to focus on evidence-based practices and be intentional in nature.

Research focusing on course design has been particularly promising. Researchers such as Levine et al. (2008) and Winkelnes et al. (2016), for instance, have found that effective course design is linked to higher levels of self-confidence among students and increased learning. Using Wiggins and McTighe's (2005) backward design approach has been found to positively impact student outcomes (Armbruster, Patel, Johnson, & Weiss, 2009; Reynolds & Kearns, 2017). The classroom is one of the best places to positively impact student retention and achievement, the ultimate goals of Guided Pathways. However, course design cannot be addressed in isolation; it must be viewed through the lens of program outcomes. As Harrington and Thomas (2018) note, course learning goals must connect to program learning goals.

The Community College Research Center (CCRC) has identified several practices that are critical to ensuring that students are having a meaningful learning experience. First, emphasis must shift from courses to programs, with a focus on program learning outcomes that meet the needs of transfer institutions and employers. The infusion of practical skills across the curriculum is necessary to ensure that students are prepared to succeed educationally and vocationally. Critical and innovative thinking, written and oral communication abilities, and computational competencies are skills that employers and upper-division institutions are demanding of graduates.

Next, there must be varied opportunities for students to use these skills through experiences such as service learning, writing-intensive courses, learning communities, internships, capstone projects, student leadership programs, and first-year experience seminars. Lastly, there must be a genuine assessment of program learning outcomes that leads to pedagogical changes that promote students' acquisition of the skills needed to be successful in future educational pursuits or the workplace (Johnstone & Karandjeff, 2017).

Helping Students Choose a Path

Colleges and universities have always asked students to select a major or path. This is not new. However, in many cases, students have not been provided with much, if any, support for making this important decision. Students who had difficulty deciding were designated undecided or exploratory. Again, very limited support has traditionally been provided to students who are unsure about which career path to pursue. Most colleges and universities offer advising or counseling, but these services are almost always optional and the students who need these services the most may never take advantage of these services.

Guided Pathways is about ensuring that all students are supported as they begin their college experience. In particular, colleges and universities using the Guided Pathways approach will often require students to meet with an advisor to discuss their career goals and to develop an educational plan. Another approach that allows students to engage in deeper career exploration and planning is to address these issues in a required first-year seminar course. One of the essential components of Guided Pathways is to move away from optional and toward mandatory advising and career conversations.

Guided Pathways is a reform movement. It was designed to capitalize on an institution's existing resources and package them in new ways to provide students with a coherent framework that allows them to efficiently move from program selection to graduation. This may require significant revisions to processes and procedures; however institutions do not need to necessarily reinvent the wheel. An assessment of established practices should lead to restructuring or modifying, where needed. Colleges should begin by analyzing how they bring students into their institution and identifying critical points during the on-boarding process where interventions can help students make meaningful choices. At most institutions, there are four opportunities for reaching large numbers of incoming students: orientation, advising, registration, and first-year seminar courses.

Orientation

New student orientation provides one of the first opportunities to introduce students to Guided Pathways concepts. Orientation is one of the 13 high-impact practices identified by the Center for Community College Student Engagement (CCCSE) as having a positive impact on student outcomes. In particular, orientation has been shown to relate to the following outcomes: completion of at least one developmental education course with a grade of C or better, completion of at least one "gatekeeper" course with a grade of C or better, and persistence, both fall-to-spring and fall-to-fall (Center for Community College Student Engagement, 2014).

Most, if not all, colleges that are national leaders in the Guided Pathways movement share similar orientation practices. While schools adapt their respective orientation programs to meet the needs of their incoming students, it should be noted that most Guided Pathways institutions have made orientation mandatory. To ensure that every student participates in orientation, many colleges such as Coastline Community (California), Pueblo Community College (Colorado), and Guilford Technical Community College (North Carolina) offer online orientation programs.

Other schools offer traditional on-campus orientation programs but supplement them with online components. For example, the Community College of Aurora (Colorado) has students complete an online introductory interest test prior to orientation. San Jacinto College (Texas) requires students to complete the Focus 2 Career Assessment and Planning tool as part of the orientation process. In preparation for orientation, Butte College (California) requires students to view online videos on topics including classroom etiquette, counseling, and navigating the college's registration portal.

Some orientation programs are organized around educational pathways, as is the case at the Community College of Aurora (Colorado), while other schools, like Lansing Community College (Michigan) introduce the concept of meta-majors during orientation. The extent to which students can manage their on-boarding experience varies among institutions. At Guilford Technical Community College (North Carolina) students can monitor their application status, activate their account, participate in pre-orientation, and access online modules.

Orientations vary from institution to institution and can range from single events to ongoing and highly organized events. Regardless of format, they are essential to helping students acclimate to college and serve as a springboard to the other on-boarding aspects of Guided Pathways. As institutions assess their orientation programs through the Guided Pathways lens, they need to be asking questions such as these:

* Should orientation be mandatory or voluntary?
* Should it be required of all students or select populations?
* How often should orientation be offered?
* What topics should be covered?
* How will the learning outcomes be assessed?
* What types of delivery modes should be used? (Achieving the Dream, n.d., p. 23)

Considering these factors during the redesign of an orientation program will help to establish Guided Pathways principles from the outset.

Advising

Academic advising is at the center of many recent discussions surrounding Guided Pathways. Academic advising often coincides with orientation or follows immediately afterward and then is, of course, ongoing throughout a student's college experience. Advising is integral to Guided Pathways; yet one of the challenges related to advising is getting more students to meet with an academic advisor and use their colleges' academic advising re-sources. This is especially true of community college students. In a national survey of entering students, less than half (44%) of the respondents reported that an advisor had helped them set academic goals and create a plan for achieving them (Center for Community College Student Engagement, 2016). This is antithetical to the philosophy of Guided Pathways.

Building intentional advising interventions into students' educational ex-periences is a primary goal of Guided Pathways. To address the high student-to-advisor ratios and the high levels of student need that are commonplace in broad-access institutions, colleges are using technology to reform their advis-ing and student support services. Commonly referred to as iPASS (integrated planning and advising systems) or technology-mediated advising, it is an integrated and multi-faceted approach to student support services. It guaran-tees that all students have access to continuous, individualized support that meets their unique needs inside and outside the classroom. Through the incorporation of data, technology, and interpersonal interactions, the ap-proach supports sweeping changes to structures, processes, attitudes, and values associated with student support services (Achieving the Dream, n.d).

Technology-mediated advising is a strategy meant to address the low completion rates associated with under-resourced advising and student sup-port services (Karp, Kalamkarian, Klampin, & Fletcher, 2016, p. 6). This advising redesign strategy uses an advisor-as-teacher approach and promotes regular contact with students along with just-in-time connections to the re-sources and information that students need. Further, it stresses educational planning by utilizing program maps and regular tracking of students' aca-demic progress (Karp et al., 2016, p.7). Technology-mediated advising oper-ationalizes two of the four Guided Pathways objectives: helping students select and begin a program pathway and keeping students on the path to graduation (Achieving the Dream, n.d., p. 13).

As institutions assess their advising processes through the Guided Path-ways lens, they need to be asking the following questions:

- How is academic advising structured?
- How are advisors assigned?
- What types of advising policies are in place?
- How do students access academic advising?
- Is advising mandatory or voluntary?
- How are advising sessions structured?
- Are various student populations advised differently?
- How do advisors utilize academic and career plans?
- How is student progress tracked?
- How is advising defined and assessed?

• What type of mandatory or voluntary training and professional development for advisors is needed? (Achieving the Dream, n.d.)

Doing so will help create an advising system that can support students not
only upon entry to the college, but as they progress toward graduation.

Colleges and universities fully engaged in Guided Pathways often use the
SSIPP model of redesigning supports. The SSIPP advising and student support redesign model uses an approach that is *sustained*, *strategic*, *integrated*,
proactive, and *personalized* (Karp & Stacey, 2013; Achieving the Dream,
n.d). In other words, advising and student supports need to be provided at key
points throughout the student's college experience when students need the
support the most. Colleges and universities can no longer wait for students to
access support. Instead, colleges and universities need to be proactive, using
technology to determine when students may need assistance. Finally, personalized online and in-person resources will increase the likelihood that students will meet with success.

Registration

Guided Pathways reform has had a significant impact on registration processes. Until recently, the mission of community colleges and broad-access four-
year institutions was clear: provide access to individuals who might not
otherwise have the opportunity to attend college. This enrollment-driven
philosophy ignored student completion and student success measures. Instead, it relied on a cafeteria-style, self-service model where students were
left on their own to select from of a myriad of disjointed courses, programs,
and services in the hopes that they would make choices that would result in
the achievement of their academic and career goals (Bailey et al., 2015).
Research has shown that this model had done little to help students realize
their objectives. As completion-driven philosophies take hold, colleges need
to consider how to align their registration processes to the Guided Pathways
framework.

Registration cannot be viewed in purely transactional terms. Within the
Guided Pathways framework, the final act of registering for classes is pre-
ceded by a series of intentional interactions designed to help students make
informed course selections. Registration is not a singular activity. It represents the culmination of those interactions and is part of what Achieving the
Dream (n.d.) refers to as an "integrated student support approach" (p. 8). It is
closely connected to advising and often leverages technology to confirm that
students are on track to meet their academic and career goals.

When bringing an integrated student support approach to scale, technology can provide information and data to increase students' efficacy and own-
ership over their educational experience, arm faculty and staff with informa-

tion that will forge more solid relationships with students, and inform strategic decision making and improve policies and procedures (Achieving the Dream, n.d., p. 11). There are numerous higher education technology solutions available today. Many of them are comprehensive registration systems that complement an integrated student support approach. Students can use these visual and interactive online registration tools to plan their future semester course schedules, build a timeline for completing program requirements, register for courses, and receive online academic advising support, while advisors, counselors, and student success coaches can monitor students' progress toward program completion.

These tools are meant to supplement, not replace, regular interactions with student support professionals. When designed and implemented properly, technology tools can provide a wealth of data and free up staff so that they can have more meaningful and impactful conversations with students.

The University of Hawaii's STAR system is an example of how technology can enhance the advising process. STAR is an in-house degree planning, audit, and registration system based on Guided Pathways principles. Implemented in 2017, it exemplifies how inclusive technology design and implementation strategies elicit transformative change from transactional processes. The system contains pre-made academic plans that give students the ability to move courses around to suit their needs. Through the "what if" feature, students can explore the impact a change of major will have on their graduation and transfer plans. An important goal of STAR was to "turn the monitor around" so that students and advisors are working in the same tool (Veney & Sugimoto, 2017). By doing so, students can take charge of the academic planning process during meetings with their advisor whether it be in person, over the phone, or through email.

Career exploration and major verification components are part of the registration feature and provide students with an extra level of assurance when making important registration decisions. The system also makes real-time registration failure data (incorrect classes, missing prerequisites, full classes, etc.) available to advisors, administrators, and faculty through a dashboard so that they can alert students when corrective action is necessary or make adjustments to the master schedule to accommodate students' needs. This example illustrates the positive effects technology can have when implemented comprehensively and inclusively within the Guided Pathways framework (Veney & Sugimoto, 2017).

To the extent possible, technology should be used to identify courses with high enrollment or courses that are canceled for low enrollment. Tracking enrollment patterns can inform decisions regarding master schedules to ensure that students are able to register for the classes they want at the times they are needed.

First-Year Seminar Courses

First-year seminar courses have also been identified by the Center for Community College Student Engagement (CCCSE) as one of the 13 high-impact practices that improve student outcomes (2014). Most colleges and universities offer some type of first-year seminar course (Young & Hopp, 2014). As an established course on most college campuses, it is an efficient means by which to reach large numbers of incoming students. After students are initially oriented, advised, and registered, first-year seminar courses can continue the on-boarding process by providing extended support throughout a new student's first semester.

First-year seminar courses typically help incoming students adjust to the demands of college by covering such topics as goal setting, time management, study skills, test-taking strategies, and note-taking techniques. Most courses also introduce students to the various support services that are available to them. First-year seminar instructors often work collaboratively with other professionals on campus. For instance, an overview of services offered by financial aid counselors, student life directors, librarians, tutors, and counselors is often integrated into the curriculum.

It is not uncommon for students in first-year seminar courses to participate in group advising sessions that are designed specifically for the class. These sessions teach students the value of being proactive and registering early for the upcoming semester. In addition, students learn about the structure of undergraduate curriculum requirements and how to best navigate academic planning and registration processes. At some institutions, first-year seminar students may receive priority registration status if they attend such a session. These interventions can improve retention and persistence rates.

Colleges may offer first-year seminar courses that are aligned to meta-majors or career clusters. In other words, different versions of the course may be offered to students majoring in business versus students majoring in the sciences. Some may offer a version of the course that is designed for undecided students, while others may offer a generic version that is open to all students, irrespective of major. Whatever the version, career exploration discussions that begin during the on-boarding process are often expanded upon in the class. In fact, first-year seminar courses, especially those aligned with Guided Pathways, often have a learning outcome specifically focused on career exploration and decision-making.

The overarching goal of the first-year seminar course is to help students establish and practice strategies and habits that will contribute to their academic and career success. Given that so many aspects of the first-year seminar course are directly aligned to the goals of Guided Pathways, it is often identified as one of the established resources that can be readily adapted to advance an institution's Guided Pathways work. The first-year seminar can be viewed as an essential foundational element of Guided Pathways.

Helping Students Stay on a Path

As students move beyond their first semester, it is increasingly imperative that a campus-wide Guided Pathways network is in place to ensure that they stay on track to meet their educational and career goals. The foundational work that takes place during the on-boarding process and in the first-year seminar course must be continually reinforced through intentional interventions at key points in a student's academic journey. Between 2009 and 2014, the overall persistence rate for first-time college students who returned to any college for their second year dropped 1.2 percentage points (National Student Clearinghouse Research Center, 2014). Many institutional efforts are aimed at first-semester students and there is little focus on supporting students throughout their educational experience.

Academic and Personal Support

The first-year seminar provides a strong foundation for success in future classes. With a focus on essential skills such as time management and study strategies, students are equipped to tackle challenging tasks ahead. Studies such as the one conducted by Karp, Raufman, Efhimiou, and Ritze (2015) investigated whether the benefits could last up to two years and found that indeed the benefits are long-lasting. To build on this foundation and support students throughout their academic journey, additional supports will likely be needed. In other words, the first-year seminar course should be an essential part of supportive programs provided to students throughout their college experience.

Often times, student support becomes less extensive because resources are limited. Many colleges and universities have decided to use their limited resources to provide higher levels of support during the first semester. While these supports are very valuable during the first-semester, ongoing support is still needed. Between 1994 and 2014, more than 31 million students enrolled in college and left without earning a degree or certificate. Nearly one-third of these students were enrolled at one institution for only one semester (Shapiro et al. 2014).

Technological tools are often necessary to bring Guided Pathways to scale on most campuses. Even so, they are not meant to replace the interpersonal interactions that are integral to each student's education experience. When used as part of a comprehensive approach to student success, technology can be the bridge that quickly connects at-risk students with the personalized assistance they need.

In other words, technology can be used to help identify those who need some type of support and intervention. Technology tools can also be used to help colleges and universities determine what types of support students need and when these supports are needed. Advisors or other student services professionals can then reach out to students. Support that is individualized and based on student needs will be most helpful. All students do not need the same level or type of support.

Early alert systems are a common example of how technology can be used to proactively reach out to students who may need support. Faculty can use the system to identify students who are struggling academically in the beginning weeks of the semester. Student support staff who are responsible for monitoring the system and supporting students can then act on these notices. Through personal contact with the student, student development specialists can determine what kind of help is needed and make arrangements for the student to receive assistance. Open lines of communication between faculty and student support professionals and a willingness to use the available tools to share information between the academic and student affairs divisions are crucial components of the Guided Pathways movement.

Ongoing Advising

Students and faculty routinely report that advising is the most important student service that colleges offer. Data from the Center for Community College Student Engagement (CCCSE) suggest that students who receive more advising, in terms of number of sessions or length of the sessions, are more engaged (Center for Community College Student Engagement, 2018). While the advising that takes place during the on-boarding process is critical to helping students choose a path, the advising that takes place as they progress through a program of study is critical to helping them stay on the path.

Program maps along with regular, intentional advising throughout a student's academic journey are essential to keeping them focused on the end goal. When meeting with students, advisors can refer to student educational and career plans that were developed in the first-year seminar. In other words, advisors can use plans to determine if students are on track to achieve their goals.

Students can fall off their path for any number of reasons: failure of a gateway course, unavailability of a required course, scheduling conflicts, and changes in their personal lives, to name a few. Challenges like these can easily deter a student; but when they routinely work with an advisor, students learn that solutions exist to problems that may have previously seemed insurmountable. With an expert on their side, not only do they stay on track, they hone the critical thinking and problem-solving skills that will serve them well both inside and outside of the classroom. Research has shown that students who meet with an advisor regularly are more likely to continue in college (Ryan, 2013) and have higher grade point averages (Kot, 2014).

Transfer and Career Assistance

Transfer assistance is also part of helping students meet with success on their path. While transfer information is of interest to many community college students, students at four-year institutions may be continuing their education as graduate students. It is important for students to know how the courses they are taking now will help prepare them for success at their transfer institution or in graduate school. Knowing this information can help students choose courses that are either required at the next educational level or will serve as foundational courses that will increase success.

To assist students with understanding the transfer process, most colleges have well-developed web pages that provide detailed information on articulation, as well as data on the top transfer destinations of graduates. Some colleges and state-wide systems have developed program maps for their most popular transfer programs and transfer destinations; however, transfer specialists can assist students with understanding the transfer process. Students will want to maximize their transfer credit upon graduation. Instant decision days and transfer fairs are popular activities at many community colleges and can serve as a motivating factor for students who are nearing graduation.

Continued career exploration is necessary if students are to stay on their path and realize their end goal. Career exploration and planning is an ongoing process. The exploration that takes place in the first-year seminar jump starts this process, but students will need further guidance throughout their college experience. For example, students who have identified a general career pathway may need to engage in deeper exploration to determine specific careers to pursue.

Toward this end, students will likely need to meet with advisors, counselors, and faculty to engage in further self-assessment related to career and to also access pertinent career information. Career professionals and faculty can assist students with conducting informational interviews and accessing learning opportunities such as job shadowing and internships. Faculty in the field can serve as mentors and help students make connections to professionals in the field and bring attention to important networking opportunities such as an upcoming conference or event. As students approach the graduation finish line, they will also likely need support with applying for positions in their field of interest.

One of the hallmarks of Guided Pathways is the concept of contextualized learning, which enables students to apply the skills they acquire in the classroom to real-world experiences. Internships, cooperative education programs, service learning, and clinical placements are some of the ways that students can use the knowledge they are acquiring in school before they graduate. Some colleges have instituted mandatory cooperative education courses or service learning components within programs to ensure that students are fully engaged in the course content. These types of experiences offer students networking opportunities that can support them during their studies and after graduation.

Capstone courses, career exploration units in first-year seminar courses, and portfolio projects are other ways colleges provide students with opportunities to synthesize program material or demonstrate competency in a subject area. Opportunities such as these provide students with a deeper and more meaningful understanding of their course material, help them confirm their career choice, enhance their resume, and enable them to experience what the future holds in store for them when they graduate.

In summary, Guided Pathways is a comprehensive reform effort aimed at improving student outcomes. Helping students choose a path and stay on a path are essential components. Although there are numerous important approaches to redesigning supports provided to students, the first-year seminar should be viewed as a foundational element of Guided Pathways. This book will focus on how the first-year seminar can be used to help students choose a path and develop the essential skills needed to be successful along their chosen path.

REFERENCES

Abel, J. R., & Dietz, R. (2014). Do the benefits of college still outweigh the costs? *Current Issues in Economics & Finance, 20(*3), 1–12. Retrieved from Academic Search Premiere.

Achieving the Dream. (n.d.). *Integrated student support redesign: A toolkit for redesigning advising and student services to effectively support every student.* Retrieved from http://achievingthedream.org/resource/17257/integrated-student-support-redesign-toolkit

Armbruster, P., Patel, M., Johnson, E., & Weiss, M. (2009). Active learning and student-centered pedagogy improve student attitudes and performance in introductory biology. *CBE Life Sciences Education, 8*(3), 203–213.

Bailey, T. R., Jaggars, S. S., & Jenkins, D. (2015). *Redesigning America's community colleges.* Cambridge, MA: Harvard University Press.

Bidwell, A. (2014). *Average student loan debt approaches $30,000.* US News. Retrieved from: https://www.usnews.com/news/articles/2014/11/13/average-student-loan-debt-hits-30-000

Center for Community College Student Engagement (2014). *A matter of degrees: Practices to pathways.* Retrieved from https://postsecondary.gatesfoundation.org/wp-content/uploads/2014/09/CCSSE-Report_Matter_of_Degrees_3.pdf

Center for Community College Student Engagement (2016). *Expectations meet reality: The underprepared student and community colleges.* Retrieved from https://www.ccsse.org/docs/Underprepared_Student.pdf

Center for Community College Student Engagement (2018). *Show me the way: The power of advising in community colleges.* Retrieved from http://www.ccsse.org/NR2018/Show_Me_The_Way.pdf

Center for Student Success at the New Jersey Council of County Colleges (n.d.) *A Guided Pathways framework.* Retrieved from http://www.njstudentsuccess.com

Complete College America (2012). *Remediation: Higher education's bridge to nowhere.* Retrieved from https://www.insidehighered.com/sites/default/server_files/files/CCA%20 Remediation%20ES%20FINAL.pdf

Complete College America. (2018). *Data Dashboard.* Retrieved from https://completecollege.org/data-dashboard/

Dann-Messier, B., Wu, P., & Greeenburg, M. (2014, May 30). *Dear colleagues letter.* Washington, DC, United States Departments of Education, Labor, and Health and Human Services. Retrieved from https://www2.ed.gov/about/offices/list/ovae/pi/cte/may-30-2014-dear-colleague-letter-career-counseling.pdf

Denley, T. (n.d.). *Choice architecture, academic foci and guided pathways.* (Tennessee Board of Regents Technical Brief No. 2.) Tennessee Board of Regents, Office of the Vice Chancellor for Academic Affairs. Retrieved from https://www.tbr.edu/sites/tbr.edu/files/media/2016/12/TBR%20Focus%20Study%202015-16.pdf

Fink, J. (2017). *What do students think of guided pathways?* (CCRC Research Brief No. 66). New York, NY: Columbia University, Teachers College, Community College Research Center.

Harrington, C., & Thomas, M. (2018). *Designing a motivational syllabus: Creating a learning path for student engagement.* Sterling, VA: Stylus.

Inside Track. (2015, January 20). *National study of non-first-time students shows full-time enrollment may not be appropriate for all* (press release). Portland, OR: Author.

Jenkins, D. (2014, June 23). *Start with the end in mind: Building guided pathways to student success.* [PowerPoint slides]. Retrieved from https://ccrc.tc.columbia.edu/media/k2/attachments/ivy-tech-summit-2014-guided-pathways.pdf

Jenkins, D., & Cho, S-W. (2014). *Get with the program . . . and finish it: Building guided pathways to accelerate student completion.* (CCRC Working Paper No. 66). Community College Research Center, Teachers College, Columbia University. Retrieved from http://ccrc.tc.columbia.edu/media/k2/attachments/get-with-the-program-and-finish-it-2.pdf

Jenkins, D., Lahr, H., & Fink, J. (2017a). *Implementing Guided Pathways: Early insights from the AACC Pathways colleges.* New York, NY: Columbia University, Teachers College, Community College Research Center.

Jenkins, D., Lahr, H., & Fink, J. (2017b). *Building blocks: Laying the groundwork for guided pathways reform in Ohio.* New York, NY: Columbia University, Teachers College, Community College Research Center.

Johnstone, R. (2015). *Guided Pathways demystified: Exploring ten commonly asked questions about implementing pathways.* National Center for Inquiry and Improvement. Retrieved from http://ncii-improve.com/publications/

Johnstone, R., & Karandjeff, K. (2017). *Guided pathways demystified II: Addressing 10 new questions as the movement gains momentum.* National Center for Inquiry and Improvement. Retrieved from http://ncii-improve.com/wp-content/uploads/2017/09/GP-Demystified-II-091517.pdf

Kantrowitz, M. (2012). *Can a student be cut off from financial aid after taking too many credits?* Retrieved from https://www.fastweb.com/financial-aid/articles/can-a-student-be-cut-off-from-financial-aid-after-taking-too-many-credits

Karp, M. M., Kalamkarian, H. S., Klampin, S., & Fletcher, J. (2016). *How colleges use integrated planning and advising for student success (iPASS) to transform student support.* (CCRC Working Paper No.89). New York, NY: Columbia University, Teachers College, Community College Research Center.

Karp, M. M., Raufman, J., Efthimiou, C., & Ritze, N. (2015). *Redesigning a student success course for sustained impact: Early outcomes findings.* (CCRC Working Paper No. 81). New York, NY: Columbia University, Teachers College, Community College Research Center.

Karp, M., & Stacey, G. W. (2013). *What we know about nonacademic student supports.* Community College Research Center, Teachers College: Columbia University.

Katz, S. N. (March 25, 2012). Beware big donors. The Chronicle of Higher Education. Retrieved from https://www.chronicle.com/article/Big-Philanthropys-Role-in/131275

Kot, F. C. (2014). The impact of centralized advising on first-year academic performance and second-year enrollment behavior. *Research in Higher Education, 55*(6), 527–563. doi: 10.1007/s11162-013-9325-4

Lederman, D. (2015, September 1). Accreditation will change—but survive. Inside Higher Ed. Retrieved from https://www.insidehighered.com/news/2015/09/01/accreditation-will-change-survive

Levine, L. E., Fallahi, C. R., Nicoll-Senft, J. M., Tessier, J. T., Watson, C. L., & Wood, R. M. (2008). Creating significant learning experiences across disciplines. *College Teaching, 56*(4), 247–254.

Lumina Foundation. (2016, April). *A stronger nation.* Indianapolis, IN: Author.

McFarland, J., Hussar, B., de Brey, C., Snyder, T., Wang, X., Wilkinson-Flicker, S., et al. (2017). *The Condition of Education 2017* (NCES 2017-144). U.S. Department of Education. Washington, DC: National Center for Education Statistics. Retrieved from https://nces.ed.gov/pubsearch/pubsinfo.asp?pubid=2017144

Mullin, C. M. (2010, June). *Rebalancing the mission: The community college completion challenge.* (AACC Policy Brief 2010-02PBL). Retrieved from https://files.eric.ed.gov/fulltext/ED522995.pdf

National Student Clearinghouse Research Center (Spring 2014). *Snapshot report: Persistence-Retention.* Retrieved from https://nscresearchcenter.org/wp-content/uploads/SnapshotReport14-PersistenceRetention-.pdf

Reynolds, H. L., & Kearns, K. D. (2017). A planning tool for incorporating backward design, active learning, and authentic assessment in the college classroom. *College Teaching, 65*(1), 17–27.

Ryan, M. (2013). Improving retention and academic achievement for first-time students at a two-year college. *Community College Journal of Research & Practice, 37*(2), 130–134. doi: 10.1080./10668926.2012.715266

Shapiro, D., Dundar, A., Yuan, X., Harrell, A., Wild, J., & Ziskin, M. (2014, July). Some College, No Degree: A National View of Students with Some College Enrollment, but No Completion (Signature Report No. 7). Herndon, VA: National Student Clearinghouse Research Center.

Snyder, T. (2014, November 5). Drawbacks of "15 to finish" [blog post]. HuffPost The Blog. Retrieved from https://www.huffingtonpost.com/tom-snyder/drawbacks-of-15-to-finish_1_b_5768788.html

Sorcinelli, M. D., Berg, J. J., Bond, H., & Watson, C. E. (2017). Why now is the time for evidence-based faculty development. In C. Haras, S. C. Taylor, M. D. Sorcinelli, and L. von Hoene (Eds.), *Institutional commitment to teaching excellence.* Washington, DC: American Council on Education.

Veney, R. M. & Sugimoto, L. H. (2017, June 19). *Transforming higher education: The guided pathways approach.* EDUCAUSE Review. Retrieved from https://er.educause.edu/articles/2017/6/transforming-higher-education-the-guided-pathways-approach

Wiggins, G., & McTyhe, J. (2005). *Understanding by design* (expanded 2nd ed.). Upper Saddle River, NJ: Pearson.

Winkelmes, M., Bernacki, M., Butler, J., Zochowski, M., Golanics, J., & Weavil, K. H. (2016). A teaching intervention that increases underserved college students' success. *Peer Review, 18*(1–2), 31–36.

Yang, D. G., & Hopp, J. M. (2014). *2012–2013 National Survey of First-Year Seminars: Exploring high-impact practices in the first college year* (Research Report No. 4). Columbia, SC: University of South Carolina, National Resource Center for the First-Year Experience and Students in Transition.

Youth Truth Student Survey (2018). *Learning from student voice: College and career readiness 2016.* Retrieved from http://www.youthtruthsurvey.org/college-and-career-readiness/

Chapter Two

History and Value of the First-Year Seminar Course

The first-year seminar is a course offered by most colleges and universities. In fact, it is often a course that is required of all or some first-year students (Young & Hopp, 2014). Throughout the years, this course has had several different purposes such as helping students transition to the college environment and helping students develop study skills that will serve them well in college. Today, many different variations of the course exist. In this chapter, an overview of the history of this course, along with current trends and the future of the course, will be discussed. In addition, the extensive research on the first-year seminar will be reviewed.

THE FIRST-YEAR SEMINAR COURSE: PAST, PRESENT, AND FUTURE

Colleges and universities have long recognized the importance of assisting students with transitioning from high school to college. As a result, colleges and universities have developed and implemented many different programs and services to support students. Orientation programs, for instance, have been designed to assist new students with establishing connections, learning about resources and opportunities available at the college or university, and understanding college expectations. Although programs such as orientation are beneficial (Mayhew, Vanderlinden, & Kim, 2010), colleges and universities recognize that these time-limited interventions are often not enough.

More in-depth structured student experiences that are longer in duration are often needed to help students meet with success. The first-year seminar is one solution that can provide students with significant, meaningful support

throughout the first semester. In fact, the first-year seminar has been identified as a high-impact practice in education (American Association of Colleges & Universities, 2008).

First-year seminar courses have a long history in the annals of higher
education and have been referred to by a variety of titles: first-year experience, freshman seminar, student success, college success, and new student
seminar, to name a few. While Kentucky's Lee College was among the first
to offer the first-year seminar course in 1882, widespread acceptance of these
courses did not take hold until the latter part of the 20th century (University
101 Programs, 2002).

Barefoot (as cited in Young & Hopp, 2014) identified four different types
of first-year seminar courses. The extended orientation first-year seminar is
one of the most common types of seminars. This type of seminar focuses on
transition issues and helping first-year students successfully adjust to the
college environment. Topics typically covered in the extended orientation
first-year seminar include campus resources, time management, career planning, study strategies, as well as other developmental concerns or issues.

There are two academic-themed types of first-year seminars: academic-
uniform and academic-variable content. First-year seminars with an academic-uniform approach are typically focused on building core academic skills
such as critical thinking and writing. With academic-uniform first-year seminars, the curriculum is usually standardized across sections. Academic-variable content courses also typically target essential academic skills, but the
focus of the course can vary by themes or topics. For example, a college or
university could offer numerous first-year seminars based on different interest areas. In this case, the curriculum could vary significantly from section to
section.

Finally, the fourth category of first-year seminars is study skills, where
the focus of the course is on helping students develop effective study habits
in order to successfully meet the academic challenges they will face in college. In a study skills first-year seminar, students will typically learn how to
engage in effective note-taking, reading, studying, and test-taking.

Although first-year seminars have always varied from institution to institution, some historical trends can be identified. Initially, first-year seminars
were designed to help academically underprepared students succeed (Ryan &
Glenn, 2004). Bogart (1994) notes that the rise in enrollment of nontraditional students, especially at community colleges, in part led to a focus on building academic skills. As nontraditional students have been out of the classroom for a number of years, many students lacked the academic skills necessary to succeed in college-level work (Boudreau & Kromrey, 1994). The
work of Pauk and Robinson significantly influenced the curriculum, with
early first-year seminars focusing on reading and study skills (Ryan & Glenn,
2004).

Enrollment challenges also contributed to the need for first-year seminars. There was a decrease in the number of high school graduates. This played a huge role in the lower enrollment rates. Because fewer students were enrolling, colleges and universities needed to focus more attention on retention and persistence. Many looked to the first-year seminar as a retention strategy. The first-year seminar was viewed as an opportunity to build essential study skills that students needed to be successful in college. As a result, more colleges instituted first-year seminar courses as a way to decrease attrition by strengthening students' learning skills. In fact, requiring a first-year seminar course of all students became much more commonplace (Ryan & Glenn, 2004).

Although first-year seminar courses targeting academic skill development were beneficial, it soon became apparent that academic skills, while important, were not enough to ensure that students met with success and completed academic programs. A significant body of research on the importance of students feeling a sense of belonging and connection to the institution emerged from the literature (Ryan & Glenn, 2004). Kuh, Kinzie, Buckley, Bridges, and Hayek (2006), for instance, noted that "students who find something or someone worthwhile to connect with in the postsecondary environment are more likely to engage in educationally purposeful activities during college, persist, and achieve their educational objectives" (p. 3). Colleges and universities turned their attention to helping students acclimate to the college environment and feel a part of the college community.

Recognizing the need for an increased focus on connection and sense of belonging, many colleges and universities shifted the focus of first-year seminar courses to transitional topics. In other words, the first-year seminar course was viewed as an extended orientation (Ryan & Glenn, 2004). With this extended orientation approach, students would typically be introduced to the many campus resources available in hopes of helping students connect to the institution. In addition, topics such as substance abuse awareness, relationships, and financial planning were typically addressed in first-year seminar courses with an extended orientation approach. Class sizes would typically be small so that students could build strong connections to their peers and their instructors.

Not surprisingly, the pendulum continues to shift. Although connection was still viewed as important, many colleges and universities shifted attention back toward academic skill development. This shift stems from the fact that many students were once again entering college without the academic skills that are needed for success and the data on the effectiveness of first-year seminars with an academic focus.

For example, in 2013, nearly one-third of the high school graduates who had taken the ACT tests were not ready for entry-level college courses in reading, English, mathematics, or science. Of the 1.8 million high school students who took the tests, only 26% attained the college readiness bench-marks in all four subject areas, with 27% meeting two or three benchmarks, and 16% meeting just one benchmark (Bidwell, 2013). That same year, the National Assessment of Educational Progress which has conducted long-term assessments on the academic performance of 9-, 13-, and 17-year-old students, reported that 17-year-old students had made no significant im-provement in reading or mathematics scores since the assessment was first administered in 1971 (National Center for Education Statistics, 2013). This lack of academic preparation among high school graduates led to an in-creased focus on developing academic skills.

There is strong research for first-year seminars with an academic focus. For example, research has shown that first-year seminars with a learning strategy focus have been found to be most effective (Ryan & Glenn, 2004). In a large-scale study of 20,031 students enrolled in transition-themed first-year seminars at 45 colleges and universities, Porter and Swing (2006) found that study skills and academic engagement had the most significant impact on students' intent to persist. In addition, first-year seminars with an academ-ic focus have been linked to improved academic performance (Permzadian & Crede, 2016).

Although first-year seminars with an extended orientation focus are still very prevalent, there has been an increase in the number of first-year semi-nars with a strong academic focus in recent years (Young & Hopp, 2014). Specifically, there was a 3.6% rise in academic uniform content and a 5.3% rise in academic variable content first-year seminars according to results of national surveys on first-year seminars conducted in 2009 and 2012 (Young & Hopp, 2014). At many colleges and universities, academic skill building has become the priority.

Today, the popularity of the first-year seminar course remains strong. The most recent survey on first-year seminars conducted by the University of South Carolina's National Resource Center for the First-Year Experience and Students in Transition, which was conducted in 2012, found that 89.7% of respondents reported offering a first-year seminar course. Thus, most col-leges and universities offer a first-year seminar course. More than half of these institutions reported requiring more than 90% of their entering students to enroll in a first-year seminar course.

Four-year colleges are much more likely to require the course of all first-year students as compared to two-year colleges (Young & Hopp, 2014). This is most likely because there is more room in a four-year curriculum and four-year colleges and universities are more likely to count the first-year seminar as part of the general education requirements. Based on survey results, 65.1% of four-year colleges count the first-year seminar as a general education requirement while only 38.6% of two-year colleges do so. At two-year colleges, the first-year seminar is often counted as an elective (Young & Hopp, 2014).

In recent years, many first-year seminar courses have a mixed approach, meaning that the curriculum includes both academic and transitional topics. Extended orientation courses are on the decline and courses that have a stronger academic focus are becoming more prevalent. However, many first-year seminar course coordinators and instructors acknowledge that the course focuses on both transitional topics such as time management and learning about campus resources as well as study skills and other success strategies. In other words, colleges and universities typically identify a combination of learning outcomes focused on both transitional and academic issues.

Cuseo (n.d.a) advocates for first-year seminars to have a holistic focus. More specifically Cuseo (n.d.a) argues that the "first-year seminar should not be referred to as "extended orientation" or even a "college transition" course. It's much more than that; it's a cross-disciplinary, holistic development course that equips students with transferable, lifelong learning skills that are applicable across the curriculum (from matriculation to graduation) and across different contexts or situations (e.g., school, work, and personal life)," (para. 4). This perspective requires a broader view of the course goals.

The world is a different place than it was decades ago when first-year seminar courses became part of the academic mainstream. Technological innovations, increased expectations of students and parents, changes to the standards of regional accrediting bodies, and stricter regulations concerning state and federal funding have raised the bar by which two- and four-year institutions are measured. It is within the context of this changing landscape that the first-year seminar must be reexamined.

It is therefore time to once again reevaluate the purpose and scope of first-year seminars. For example, first-year seminar courses are poised to serve a pivotal role in advancing the goals of the Guided Pathways movement. Juncos, Harrington, Orosz, and Suk (2017) argued that the first-year seminar can be used as a vehicle to help students choose a career pathway and develop the skills needed to successfully achieve career goals. Unfortunately, career exploration has not been historically emphasized as much as other student success topics. According to the results of a national survey, only 29.3% of the two-year colleges and 13.1% of the four-year colleges who responded to the survey indicated that career exploration and preparation was a focus of the course (Young & Hopp, 2014).

Students enrolled in a first-year seminar course can engage in deep and meaningful career exploration and then develop academic, career, and financial plans to map out the path toward success. The first-year seminar offers students an opportunity to engage in meaningful career exploration and planning throughout an entire semester rather than in just one or two visits with an advisor, counselor, or success coach. First-year seminar courses offer an effective way to introduce Guided Pathways' concepts to all entering students. This common learning experience can be used to help students engage in career exploration and to develop the skills needed to meet with success. This is the future of first-year seminar courses.

In their seminal book, *Redesigning America's Community Colleges*, Bailey, Jaggars, and Jenkins (2015) suggest narrowing the course content. Too often, first-year seminar courses are the place to address any and all content related to transitioning to college. Information deemed important for incoming students but, for various reasons, not covered during new-student orientation often finds its way into the first-year seminar course. As a result, many first-year seminar courses have been composed of a vast assortment of topics that are impossible to cover during a one-, two-, or three-credit course and may not even be aligned to the course learning outcomes. This "everything but the kitchen sink" approach to content diminishes the purpose and effectiveness of the course and presents instructional challenges that can be insurmountable.

To remedy this situation, first-year seminar course coordinators must reexamine this course based on the needs of students and current institutional priorities. Clear and focused learning outcomes must be identified and then the curriculum must align to these outcomes. Including learning outcomes that target career exploration and decision making along with developing and strengthening students' learning and success skills will undoubtedly increase student success. Revising and focusing the first-year seminar curriculum will better prepare students for the demands of college and the 21st-century workplace.

DATA AND EVIDENCE FOR THE FIRST-YEAR SEMINAR COURSE

There is strong evidence that illustrates the important role that first-year seminar courses play in student success outcomes. In fact, Cuseo (n.d.a) notes that the first-year seminar is likely the course on campus with the most national and institutional data demonstrating its effectiveness. Numerous studies have demonstrated the positive impact that first-year seminar courses have on student retention and persistence, grade point average, and degree completion (Cuseo, n.d.a; Mills, 2010; Pascarella & Terenzini, 2005; Swing, 2002). You will find infographics highlighting key research findings that support the first-year seminar in appendix A.

In addition to exploring the impact of the first-year seminar on typical outcomes such as retention, grades, and completion, researchers have also identified other benefits of the course. For example, the first-year seminar has also been shown to help students develop a strong sense of belonging to the institution (Keup & Barefoot, 2005), which has been demonstrated to be connected to success outcomes (Kuh et al., 2006). Researchers have also found that the first-year seminar assists students with making career decisions (Adams, Thomas, & McDaniel, 2008; Jaijairam, 2016). In this section, we will review the extensive literature on the effectiveness of first-year seminar courses.

Prior to reviewing the numerous studies that illustrate the value of the first-year seminar, it is important to note that most of the studies on this course are not experimental in nature. This is not unique to the first-year seminar, but rather quite typical in the field of higher education. In higher education, much research is correlational and descriptive in nature. Although causal statements cannot be made based on this type of research, increased confidence comes from carefully designed studies that used matched cohorts and consistent results across numerous studies. Researchers often compared students in first-year seminars with a matched control group of students who were similar on a variety of factors but who did not take a first-year seminar course.

Thus, caution must be exercised when reviewing the research findings. It is not appropriate to infer causation unless the data result from an experimental study. It is of course entirely possible that the differences in the students versus the course itself are the reason for the findings. However, given the fact that there is a significant body of research on the impact of the first-year seminar course and that the findings across numerous studies with very different student populations consistently have the same positive results, it is very likely that the first-year seminar is playing a critical role in improving student outcomes.

Retention and Persistence

Increasing retention has long been a goal of the first-year seminar course. There are numerous studies that illustrate that the first-year seminar is connected to persistence in college (Griffin & Romm, 2008). Students who take the first-year seminar course are more likely to persist and continue in college. For example, Dahlgren (2008) found that 63.4% of students were still in college one year after taking the first-year seminar as compared to only 45% of students who did not take the first-year seminar course. This difference is both statistically and clinically significant. In an earlier study, Bushko (1995) found that students taking a first-year seminar course at Widener University, as compared to students who did not take the course, were 18% more likely to attend college as a sophomore.

To investigate the connection between the first-year seminar and retention, Boudreau and Kromrey (1994) conducted a longitudinal study. Results revealed higher retention rates for students who enrolled in a first-year seminar course, as compared to students who had not taken the course, for two of the four years. Studies have found that these higher retention rates held true even after researchers controlled for a variety of student characteristics and their participation in support programs (Jackson, 2005).

Data from another longitudinal study conducted at a public community college in California found that over a four-year period, the average persistence rate, as defined by the number of students who returned in the subsequent semester, for students who successfully completed the institution's first-year seminar course was 85.4% as compared to 57.8% for the entire student population during that same time period (Fralick, 2008). Ben-Avie, Kennedy, Unson, Li, Ricardi, and Mugno (2012) also found the retention rate for first-year seminar participants outpaced that of non-seminar students for three years.

Permzadian and Crede (2016) conducted a meta-analysis on first-year seminars and found that first-year seminars had a small, positive effect on one-year retention rates. First-year seminars with a focus on helping students adjust, transition, and make connections at college, often referred to as extended orientation type first-year seminars, had a more positive impact on student retention.

Further evidence about persistence comes from a study conducted by Derby and Smith (2004). Results of this study found that students were more likely to return to school following a one-, two-, or three-semester break as compared to students who did not take the course. In other words, for students who stopped out of college, those who took the first-year seminar were more likely to return and continue taking courses toward their degree.

Evidence for persistence can also be measured by the number of credits earned by students. Cho and Karp (2013) utilized data from the Virginia Community College System (VCCS) to investigate credits earned in the first year and persistence to the second year. The study controlled for several student characteristics such as gender, race, age, Pell grant received, and English as a Second Language course enrollment as well as institutional characteristics such as rural, urban, or suburban locations and median instructional expenditure per student. Enrollment in a first-year seminar course was positively associated with all outcomes measured and proved to be statistically significant. As compared to students who did not enroll in a first-year seminar course, students who enrolled in the first-year seminar course within their first 15 credits were 10 percentage points more likely to earn college-level credits in their first year and 10 percentage points more likely to persist to the second year. Students who enrolled in the course within their first semester were 6 percentage points more likely to persist to year two. The study affirmed the positive relationship between first-year seminar course enrollment in the first semester and the immediate outcomes of credit attainment and persistence to the second year of college.

Academic Performance

Students who take a first-year seminar course are more likely to perform well academically. Results from a study conducted by Boudreau and Kromrey (1994) explored this issue. Results indicated that for all but one year, the average grade point average and total credits completed by the first-year seminar students exceeded that of the students who did not take the course. In another study, Dahlgren (2008) also found that students who took the first-year seminar had higher grade point averages (2.76) as compared to students who did not take the course (2.50).

The academic benefits of the first-year seminar course are strongly illustrated by studies that also assess and account for differing academic abilities of students. Schwartz and Grieve (2008), for instance, found that students who took the first-year seminar course at Lourdes College had higher grade point averages (3.04) than students who did not take the first-year seminar course (2.60). It is important to note that the students who did not take the first-year seminar course had similar high school grade point averages and ACT scores to those who did take the course (Schwartz & Grieve, 2008). In other words, students had similar academic performance prior to taking the course.

House (2005) also found that students who took a first-year seminar course at Northern Illinois University had significantly higher grade point averages at the end of the first term and first year as compared to students who did not take the first-year seminar course even after controlling for ACT scores. In a similar study, Jenkins-Guarnier, Horne, Wallis, Rings, and Vaughan (2015) found that students who successfully completed the first-year seminar had higher levels of academic performance than peers who did not take the course even after prior academic performance and first-generational status were accounted for. In other words, the grade point averages were not due to differences in academic ability. The first-year seminar likely played a significant role in improved academic performance.

Research has shown that improved academic performance can go beyond the first year. In a large-scale study of approximately 2,000 students, Jamelske (2008) found that students who took the first-year seminar course had higher grade point averages one year after taking the course than students who did not take the course. Karp, Raufman, Efhimiou, and Ritze (2015) found that semester grades were almost a half-grade higher for students who took a first-year seminar as compared to students who did not take the course and that these academic advantages lasted up to two years.

Other research has shown that the academic benefits can carry with students throughout their college career. For example, Jajairam (2016) found that "freshman who receive a high grade in FYS [first-year seminar] are more likely to achieve better grades for courses that they take when they are sophomores or juniors" (p. 21).

Further evidence that academic benefits are long-lasting comes from a study conducted at a four-year public university in the Northeast. Researchers compared academic achievement of first-year students who participated in a first-year seminar as part of a comprehensive First-Year Experience program with first-year students who, while part of the First-Year Experience program, did not take the course. Results indicated that the students who enrolled in the first-year seminar had significantly higher term and cumulative grade point averages, earned more credits, and were retained at a higher rate than the students who did not take the seminar. It is important to note that the results indicated that the academic benefits were long-lasting. The higher term grade point averages of seminar participants lasted for seven semesters. Over the same period, seminar participants also accrued more credits (Ben-Avie et al., 2012).

Based on a meta-analytic study conducted by Permzadian and Crede (2016), first-year seminars have a small, but positive effect on grade point averages. These researchers noted that some first-year seminars were effective at positively impacting academic performance while other first-year seminars were not. For example, they found that first-year seminars with an academic component or focus are more likely to result in improved academic performance than first-year seminars with an extended orientation focus.

Graduation Rates

Completing college requirements and graduating is obviously a priority for students and colleges alike. The connection between the first-year seminar and graduation rates has been explored by several researchers. After reviewing over 40 studies, Pascarella and Terenzini (2005) found that students who took the first-year seminar course were more likely to graduate within four years.

Based on a review of statewide data from the Florida community college system, Zeidenberg, Jenkins, and Calcagno (2007) found that students who took the first-year seminar course were 8% more likely than their peers who did not take the course to earn a credential. It is important to note that this research finding is based on a large sample size of over 37,000 students and that these findings were consistent even when the data were disaggregated by college preparedness, remedial course requirements, and race/ethnicity. This research emphasizes the important role the first-year seminar course plays in helping students develop skills needed to complete credentials that are valuable in the world of work.

Schnell, Louis, and Doetkott (2003) conducted a four-year study at a mid-sized, public university in the Midwest to determine if students' enrollment in a first-year seminar course had any influence on graduation. A total of 1,700 students participated in this longitudinal study. Findings were compiled after each cohort had the opportunity to complete five years of college. The four-year graduation rate for first-year seminar participants was significantly higher (16.67%) than that of nonparticipants (11.79%). The same was true for the five-year graduation rate, with 40% of the first-year seminar students graduating as compared to 32% of the students who did not enroll in the course.

Results from a three-year study at a midwestern community college also revealed a significant positive association between the students who took the first-year seminar course and those who earned a degree within the traditional two-year timeframe (Derby & Smith, 2004). In a study on commuter students, it was found that students who took the first-year seminar graduated within four years at rates higher than students who did not take the first-year seminar (Blowers & Elling, 2005). More specifically, the four-year graduation rate for students taking the course was 28% while the four-year graduation rate for students not taking the course was only 17%.

Although the graduation rates in these studies leave much to be desired, these research studies show evidence that the first-year seminar positively impacts graduation rates. In several studies, the graduation rate was significantly higher for students who participated in a first-year seminar than for students who did not participate. The first-year seminar undoubtedly helps students develop the skills needed to persist and make it to the finish line of completing a certificate or degree.

Career Decision Making

In addition to academic benefits, the first-year seminar can also assist students with career decision making. This was illustrated by Adams et al. (2008) who found that students who took the first-year seminar had higher levels of self-efficacy related to career decision making. In addition to higher career decision-making self-efficacy, students in this study also had higher levels of career decidedness after taking the first-year seminar course (Adams et al. 2008). In other words, students were confident in their decision-making skills and were more likely to make career decisions if they participated in a first-year seminar course. Career decision benefits were also noted by Jaijairam (2016) who surveyed over 500 students about their experience taking a first-year seminar. Results revealed that 85% of students who took a first-year seminar and completed the survey reported having a better sense of career options (Jaijairam, 2016).

Further support for the value of the first-year seminar related to career decision-making comes from Peterson and Stubblefield (2008). According to their research conducted at the University of Minnesota, students who took the first-year seminar reported being less uncertain about the career decision-making process. On a pre- and post-test, significant gains were observed on the following statements: "I know what careers might interest me" and "I am familiar with tools and resources for exploring majors and careers" (p. 76). More specifically, the mean score for these items went from 2.15 to 3.1 and 1.8 to 3.1, respectively (Peterson & Stubblefield, 2008).

Students, especially first-year students, appreciate the opportunity to learn about the career exploration process. In fact, in a study conducted at SUNY College at Brockport by Fox and Esler (2005), students taking a first-year seminar showed the highest interest in the course goal related to understanding career options.

In addition to discussing career decision making in class, students who take a first-year seminar course are more likely to engage in outside-of-class actions related to career decision-making. For instance, students who take a first-year seminar are more likely to report discussing career plans with a faculty member. This was illustrated in a study by Blowers and Elling (2005) where 92% of students who took a first-year seminar reported talking with a faculty member about career plans as compared to only 77% of students who did not take a first-year seminar.

Based on these findings, students who take a first-year seminar course are more likely to understand the career-decision process and feel more equipped to engage in this process. In addition, students taking a first-year seminar are more able to identify career options and are more likely to converse with a faculty member about their career options and plans. When students engage in career exploration and decision making, they are more likely to make better decisions and meet with success.

Does the First-Year Seminar Benefit All Students?

Some professionals believe that only at-risk students need to take the first-year seminar course, arguing that students of high-ability levels do not need the course and do not benefit from taking the course. However, researchers have found that students of all ability levels benefit from the course. Although Howard and Jones (2000) hypothesized that the first-year seminar would be most beneficial to students with low academic preparation, results of their study revealed the course benefited students of all ability levels. Howard and Jones (2000) noted that the data "suggests that rather than being a course for the 'under-prepared,' there is a pervasive positive impact of the course, regardless of prior preparation" (p. 515).

Miller, Janz, and Chen (2007) also investigated this issue. Specifically, these researchers were interested in determining if the benefits students derived from taking the course depended upon their level of academic preparedness when they entered college. Preparedness was measured by high school grades, high school rank, ACT scores, and the number of college preparation courses. Results of the study revealed that students of all ability levels benefited from the class.

More specifically, students with low, mid, and high academic preparation prior to arriving at college who took the first-year seminar course had higher retention and graduation rates than their peers who did not take the course. For students with low academic preparation, first-year retention rates were 93.7% for students who took the first-year seminar course as compared to only 83.8% for students who did not take the course. The first-year retention rates were 93.9% for students with mid-range academic preparation who took the course as compared to 88.6% for those who did not take the course and 96.6% for high ability students who took the course as compared to 90.6% for high ability students who did not take the course. Similar findings were revealed for graduation rates, with students of all ability levels having higher graduation rates if they took the first-year seminar course. Fourth year graduation rates were 25.1% versus 18.2% for low-ability students, 40.3% versus 26.4% for mid-range ability students, and 52.5% versus 45.1% for high-ability students, with those taking the first-year seminar graduating at higher rates (Miller et al., 2007).

In an interesting study conducted by Pittendrigh, Borkowksi, Swinford, and Plumb (2016), the impact of the first-year seminar on students with varying levels of motivation was investigated. In this study, the researchers focused on the persistence of students enrolled in an academically challenging, discussion-based first-year seminar. The seminar was open to all first-year students. Data was collected through the administration of the College Student Inventory (CSI) and a pre– and post–Knowledge and Community Seminar Survey (KCSS).

Using the results of the CSI, the College Motivation factor score was found to be the primary predictor of persistence. Students who enrolled in the first-year seminar had higher persistence rates when compared to students with higher motivation scores who did not enroll in the seminar. An analysis of the pre- and post-administration of the KCSS found that less-motivated seminar students had lower persistence rates when they did not believe college was needed to reach their career goals, disliked discussion-based classes, or did not participate in class. Less-motivated seminar students had higher persistence rates if they believed that college was needed to reach their career goals, enjoyed discussion-based classes, or actively participated in class. Based on their findings, the researchers concluded that students of all motivational levels can benefit when placed in a multidisciplinary, academically challenging first-semester seminar (Pittendrigh et al., 2016).

Permzadian and Crede (2016) conducted a meta-analytic review of first-year seminars to determine what type of first-year seminars are most effective and for whom. They found that first-year seminars were least effective when they enrolled only academically underprepared students. The efficacy of seminars improved when they were required of all incoming students. These findings are consistent with a body of literature that shows that heterogenous groups, as opposed to homogenous groups, are most likely to lead to the best outcomes (Woolfolk, 2012).

Summary of Evidence

Based on this extensive review of the literature on first-year seminars, there is strong evidence that the first-year seminar plays an important, positive role in helping students achieve success. More specifically, research has found connections between the first-year seminar course and persistence, academic performance, and graduation rates, as well as other factors such as stronger sense of belonging and increased understanding of the career exploration process. Although much of this research relies on correlations, and causal statements cannot therefore be made, it is important to note that many of these studies controlled for numerous factors associated with success and that these positive outcomes have been found across numerous studies with different student populations.

Situating the first-year seminar course within a Guided Pathways framework offers the possibility of contributing to even higher levels of successful outcomes. Karp and colleagues (2012) suggest that first-year seminar courses can contribute to improved long-term learning outcomes if the focus is on teaching students how to apply course-related skills and knowledge. This aligns with two of the four 21st-century learning outcomes identified by Keup (2013) as essential to students' first-year experience: intellectual and practical skills and integrative learning.

First-year seminar courses can provide the foundation for sustained, positive student outcomes if the content is relative to students' lives, provides them with opportunities to practice new skills, and teaches them when and how to apply their newly acquired skills and knowledge outside of the classroom (Karp et al., 2015). This focus combined with strong career exploration and planning will likely lead to even more positive and long-lasting student outcomes.

As colleges and universities reimagine the first-year seminar to align with Guided Pathways and include more extensive opportunities for career exploration, intentional academic planning, building essential skills, and connecting students to one another and the college, it is likely that outcome data will be even stronger in the future. Future researchers can investigate the effectiveness of first-year seminars in terms of traditional outcomes such as graduation and retention, but also include other variables such as career decidedness and sense of belonging. As future researchers continue to explore the effectiveness of this course, differentiating between seminars that are aligned to Guided Pathways and those that are not will also be important.

In summary, the first-year seminar has long been focused on helping students transition to college and develop essential skills needed for success. The significant body of research that supports this course describes its value in terms of traditional outcomes such as retention and graduation as well as in other important ways such as increasing the sense of belonging or connection and the career decision-making process. Reimagining the first-year seminar as a strong foundational component of Guided Pathways, focusing on both career exploration and skill development, is the next frontier.

REFERENCES

Adams, P., Thomas, J. H., & McDaniel, C. R. (2008). Northern Kentucky University. In A. M. Griffin & J. Romm (Eds.), *Exploring the evidence, Volume IV: Reporting on first-year seminars* (pp. 57–60). Columbia, SC: University of South Carolina, National Resource Center for the First-Year Experience and Students in Transition.

American Association of American Colleges & Universities (2008). *High-impact educational practices.* Retrieved from https://www.aacu.org/leap/hips

Bailey, T. R., Jaggars, S. S., & Jenkins, D. (2015). *Redesigning America's community colleges.* Cambridge, MA: Harvard University Press.

Ben-Avie, M., Kennedy, M., Unson, C., Li, J., Riccardi, R. L., & Mugno, R. (2012). First-year experience: A comparison study. *Journal of Assessment and Institutional Effectiveness, 2*(2), 143–170.

Bidwell, A. (2013, August 21). *High school graduates still struggle with college readiness.* U.S. News & World Report. Retrieved from https://www.usnews.com/news/articles/2013/08/21/high-school-graduates-still-struggle-with-college-readiness

Blowers, A. N., & Elling, T. W. (2005). University of North Carolina at Charlotte. In B. F. Tobolowsky, B. E. Cox, & M. T. Wagner (Eds.), *Exploring the evidence: Reporting on first-year seminars. Volume III (Monograph No. 42)* (pp. 175–178). Columbia, SC: University of South Carolina, National Resource Center for The First-Year Experience and Students in Transition.

Bogart, Q. J. (1994). The community college mission. In G. A. Baker III, J. Dudzia, & P. Tyler (Eds.), *A handbook on the community college in America: Its history, mission, and management* (pp. 60–73). Westport, CT: Greenwood Press.

Boudreau, C. A., & Kromrey, J. D. (1994). A longitudinal study of the retention and academic performance of participants in a freshmen orientation course. *Journal of College Student Development, 35*(6), 444–449.

Bushko, A. A. (1995). Freshman seminar improves student retention at Widener University. *Freshman Year Experience Newsletter, 8*(2), p. 9.

Cho, S., & Karp, M. M. (2013). Student success courses in the community college: Early enrollment and educational outcomes. *Community College Review, 41*(1), 86–103.

Cuseo, J. (n.d.a). What exactly is "academic rigor? Unpublished manuscript.

Cuseo, J. (n.d.b). The empirical case for the first-year seminar: Evidence of course impact on student retention, persistence to graduation, and academic achievement. Unpublished manuscript.

Dahlgren, D. (2008). Indiana University Southeast. In A. M. Griffin & J. Romm (Eds.), *Exploring the evidence, Volume IV: Reporting on first-year seminars* (pp. 21–25). Columbia, SC: University of South Carolina, National Resource Center for the First-Year Experience and Students in Transition.

Derby, D. C., & Smith T. (2004). An orientation course and community college retention. *Community College Journal of Research and Practice, 28,* 763–773.

Fox, P. M., & Esler, M. (2005). State University of New York at Brockport. In B. F. Tobolow-sky, B. E. Cox, & M. T. Wagner (Eds.), *Exploring the evidence: Reporting on first-year seminars. Volume III* (Monograph No. 42), (pp.145–149). Columbia, SC: University of South Carolina, National Resource Center for The First-Year Experience and Students in Transition.

Fralick, M. (2008). Comprehensive college success courses increase student persistence, self-confidence and satisfaction. In W. G. Troxel & M. Cutright (Eds.), *Exploring the evidence: Initiatives in the first college year* (Monograph No. 49). Columbia, SC: University of South Carolina, National Resource Center for the First-Year Experience and Students in Transition.

Griffin, A. M., & Romm, J. (2008). *Exploring the evidence, Volume IV: Reporting on first-year seminars.* Columbia, SC: University of South Carolina, National Resource Center for the First-Year Experience and Students in Transition.

House, J. D. (2005). Northern Illinois University. In B. F. Tobolowsky, B. E. Cox, & M. T. Wagner (Eds.), *Exploring the evidence: Reporting research on first-year seminars, Volume III* (Monograph No. 42), (pp. 103–106). Columbia, SC: University of South Carolina, National Resource Center for The First-Year Experience and Students in Transition.

Howard, H. E., & Jones, W. D. (2000, December). Effectiveness of a freshman seminar in an urban university: Measurement of selected indicators. *College Student Journal, 34*(4), 509–515.

Jackson, B. (2005). Indiana University-Purdue University Indianapolis. In B. F. Tobolowsky, B. E. Cox, & M. T. Wagner (Eds.), *Exploring the evidence: Reporting research on first-year seminars, Volume III* (Monograph No. 42), (pp. 61–65). Columbia, SC: University of South Carolina, National Resource Center for The First-Year Experience and Students in Transition.

Jaijairam, P. (2016). First-year seminar—The advantages that this course offers. *Journal of Education and Learning, 5*(2), 15–23. doi: 10.5539/jel.v5n2p15

Jamelske, E. (2008). Measuring the impact of a university first-year experience program on student GPA and retention. *Higher Education, 57*, 373–391.

Jenkins-Guarnieri, M. A., Horne, M. M., Wallis, A. L., Rings, J. A., & Vaughan, A. L. (2015). Quantitative evaluation of a first-year seminar program: Relationships to persistence and academic success. *Journal of College Student Retention, 16*(4), 593–606.

Juncos, A., Harrington, C., Orosz, T., & Suk, K. (2017). *The first-year seminar: An essential component of Guided Pathways.* Presented at the Annual Conference of The First-Year Experience and Students in Transition. Atlanta, GA.

Karp, M. M., Bickerstaff, S., Rucks-Ahidiana, Z., Bork, R. H., Barragan, M., & Edgecombe, N. (2012). *College 101 courses for applied learning and student success* (CCRC Working Paper No. 49). New York, NY: Columbia University, Teachers College, Community College Research Center.

Karp, M. M., Raufman, J., Efthimiou, C., & Ritze, N. (2015). *Redesigning a student success course for sustained impact: Early outcomes findings* (CCRC Working Paper No. 81). New York, NY: Columbia University, Teachers College, Community College Research Center.

Keup, J. R. (2013). *The first-year experience: Lessons learned and emerging issues.* Presentation given at the 2013 Teaching and Learning Conference. Retrieved from http://sc.edu/fye/research/research_presentations/files/Keup_Teaching%20and%20Learning%20Confer ence_Johannesburg%202013.pdf

Keup, J., & Barefoot, B. (2005). Learning how to be a successful student: Exploring the impact of first-year seminars on student outcomes. *Journal of the First-Year Experience & Students in Transition, 1*, 11–47.

Kuh, G. D., Kinzie, J., Buckley, J. A., Bridges, B. K., & Hayek, J. C. (2006). *What matters to student success: A review of the literature.* Report for the National Symposium on Postsecondary Student Success: Spearheading a Dialog on Student Success.

Mayhew, M. J., Vanderlinden, K., & Kim, E. (2010). A multi-level assessment of the impact of orientation programs on student learning. *Research in Higher Education, 51*(4), 320–345.

Miller, J. W., Janz, J. C., & Chen, C. (2007). The retention impact of a first-year seminar on students with varying pre-college academic performance. *Journal of the First-Year Experience & Students in Transition, 19*(1), 47–62.

Mills, M. T. (2010). Tools of engagement: Success course influence on student engagement. *Journal of the First-Year Experience & Students in Transition, 22*(2).

National Center for Education Statistics (2013). The Nation's Report Card: Trends in Academic Progress 2012 (NCES 2013–456). National Center for Education Statistics, Institute of Education Sciences, U.S. Department of Education, Washington, D.C.

National Resource Center for the First-Year Experience and Students in Transition (2013). *2012–2013 National survey of first-year seminars* (Executive Summary). Retrieved from http://sc.edu/fye/research/surveys/survey_instruments/pdf/Executive_Summaries_2013_National_Survey_FirstYearSeminars.pdf

O'Gara, L., Karp, M. M., & Hughes, K. L. (2009). Student success courses in the community college: An exploratory study of student perspectives. *Community College Review, 36*(3).

Pascarella, E. T. & Terenzini, P. T. (2005). *How college affects students: A third decade of research* (Vol. 2). San Francisco, CA: Jossey-Bass.

Permzadian, V., & Crede, M. (2016). Do first year seminars improve college grades and retention? A quantitative review of their overall effectiveness and an examination of moderators of effectiveness. *Review of Educational Research, 86*(1) 277–316.

Peterson, K., & Stubblefield, R. (2008). University of Minnesota. In A. M. Griffin & J. Romm (Eds.). *Exploring the evidence, Volume IV: Reporting on first-year seminars* (pp. 73–78). Columbia, SC: University of South Carolina, National Resource Center for the First-Year Experience and Students in Transition.

Pittendrigh, A., Borkowski, J., Swinford, S., & Plumb, C. (2016). Knowledge and community: The effect of a first-year seminar on student persistence. *Journal of General Education, 15*(1) 48–65.

Porter, S. R., & Swing, R. L. (2006). Understanding how first-year seminars affect persistence. *Research in Higher Education, 47*(1), 89–109.

Ryan, M. P., & Glenn, P. A. (2004). What do first-year students need most: Learning strategies instruction or academic socialization? *Journal of College Reading and Learning, 34*(2), 4–28.

Schnell, C. A., Louis, K. S., & Doetkott, C. (2003). The first-year seminar as a means of improving college graduation rates. *Journal of the First-Year Experience, 15*(1) 53–76.

Schwartz, D. & Grieve, K. (2008). In A. M. Griffin & J. Romm (Eds.). *Exploring the evidence, Volume IV: Reporting on first-year seminars* (pp. 41–44). Columbia, SC: University of South Carolina, National Resource Center for the First-Year Experience and Students in Transition.

Swing, R. L. (August 28, 2002). First-year initiative overview. The Policy Center on the First Year of College. Retrieved from http://www.brevard.edu/fyc/fyi/essays/index.htm

Thelin, J. R. (2004). *A history of American higher education.* Baltimore, MD: The Johns Hopkins University Press.

University 101 Programs (2002). *History of the first year seminar and university 101 program.* Retrieved from http://sc.edu/univ101/aboutus/history.html

Woolfolk, A. (2012). *Educational psychology* (12th edition). Boston: Pearson Education.

Young, D. G., & Hopp, J. M. (2014). *2012–2013 National Survey of First-Year Seminars: Exploring high-impact practices in the first college year* (Research Report No. 4). Columbia, SC: University of South Carolina, National Resource Center for The First-Year Experience and Students in Transition.

Zeidenberg, M., Jenkins, D., & Calcagno, J. C. (2007). Do student success courses actually help community college students succeed? *Community College Resource Center Brief, 36*, 1–6.

Chapter Three

Helping Students Choose a Career Path

The Role of the First-Year Seminar Course

Helping students choose a career path is an essential part of Guided Pathways. Many students enter college as an undecided or exploratory student, meaning they have not yet decided on a career pathway. The exact number of students in this situation is difficult to capture because many students may select a major without much thought or commitment. However, research conducted by Albion and Fogarty (2002), suggests 65–70% of students are undecided about which career pathway to pursue.

Even students who do enter college with a declared major and a related career goal sometimes change their mind and choose a different major and career path. Cuseo (n.d.) reminds us that declaring a major is not the same as committing to a major. Changing majors is more likely to occur when students have made a choice without engaging in much career exploration. In this case, the choice they made may not have been the best one.

There are a variety of reasons for career indecision. Gati, Krausz, and Osipow (1996) identified three primary reasons that students may have difficulty deciding on a career path. The three reasons are as follows: lack of readiness, lack of information, and inconsistent information. Two of these reasons relate to information; students may not have enough information about themselves or careers or may have inconsistent or conflicting information. Colleges can easily find ways to assist students with these challenges. Information literacy is often the focus of course and program learning outcomes and therefore is often emphasized in courses. The first-year seminar is a foundational course that can easily incorporate information literacy skills, especially as related to careers, into the curriculum. Information literacy skills typically develop during college.

Another reason for career indecision, identified by Gati et al. (1996), is not being ready to make this decision or having difficulties making decisions in general. In other words, students may not yet be motivated to do the work associated with engaging in career exploration or may simply struggle with making decisions. In this case, the student may have low self-efficacy related to career decision making, meaning the student does not have much confidence in his or her ability to make a career decision. Taveira and Moreno (2003) report that self-efficacy related to career decision making is an important consideration in the career exploration process. As a result, they argue that career exploration involves much more than information gathering.

Bailey, Smith Jaggars, and Jenkins (2015) argue that one reason that choosing a major and career path is so difficult is because there are too many choices. Students are faced with thousands of career options and often hundreds of majors. Having too many options can make decision making extremely difficult.

This was illustrated in a fascinating study by Iyengar and Lepper (2000) where they investigated how individuals make choices in both laboratory and field settings. More specifically, individuals were exposed to either six types of jam or approximately 30 types of jam. Findings showed that those who were only provided with six options were more likely to purchase the jam, making a decision. In this same study, Iyengar and Lepper (2000) also investigated academic choices. Students were given an opportunity to do an extra-credit paper and had either six topic options or 30 topic options. Students who were only given six topics were more likely to do the extra credit and also reported higher levels of satisfaction with their topic and performed better on the paper.

As a result of the research showing the connection between having too many choices and not deciding, Bailey et al. (2015) have encouraged colleges to consider moving toward a meta-major or career pathway framework, believing that this can be an approach that is useful to students who are undecided. A meta-major or career pathway refers to broad categories of careers such as business, education, health sciences, and liberal arts. In essence, when a meta-major approach is used by a college, students choose a meta-major or career pathway rather than a specific major upon entry into college. Instead of having to select a major from sometimes hundreds of options, students need to choose between perhaps five and ten meta-majors or career pathways. The primary advantage of this approach is that students can start taking required courses in the selected pathway as they explore the options within that area or career pathway.

However, there are some potential challenges associated with using a meta-major framework. For starters, although this is an easier task for many students, there will likely still be some students who are truly undecided. In fact, Bailey et al. (2015) note that 17% of incoming students at community colleges reported having no idea at all when asked about a major or career path. This means that almost one in five students may even have difficulty deciding on a general career pathway. In this case, having shared introductory classes in the discipline is not necessarily a benefit. Since the student is not really committed to the career pathway, it is very possible that a student may change to a completely different meta-major or career pathway.

Unfortunately, there is very limited data available related to changing majors and the research that does exist has mixed results. It can be difficult to even determine how many students change their major as not all institutions track this information in the same way and students may change their mind about a major but not officially change it with the registrar's office. The number of students who change their major probably varies significantly from institution to institution. Beggs, Bantham, and Taylor (2008) reported that 65% of the students in their study never changed their major. However, they noted that institutional obstacles for doing so may be the reason rather than students being completely committed to their original major. For instance, some majors may have highly competitive admission requirements, making switching majors for students with less than exemplary academic records a challenge.

Some research indicates that when students change their major, they often do so within the general school or college (Colorado State University, 2011). However, this is not always the case. According to a 2009 report written by the National Center for Education Statistics, 36% of students changed from a STEM to a non-STEM major. Thus, some students are making more significant changes to different career pathways.

Drysdale, Frost, and McBeath (2015) investigated why students change their major and discovered that approximately 30% of students changed their major because they developed new interests, 23% did so because of dissatisfaction with their current major, and 14% of students reported changing their major because the program was too difficult.

Interestingly, Micceri (2001) found that changing majors was associated with higher graduation rates as compared to students who did not change majors. This seems counter-intuitive. Perhaps students who change their majors are more engaged in career exploration and as a result, end up having a higher level of commitment to the career pathway selected. If students are changing their major because they are no longer enjoying their current major or are finding it to be too difficult, as indicated by Drysdale et al. (2015), then it makes sense that changing majors could have more positive outcomes.

However, it is important to note that others have found that changing a major can mean that students may take longer to get to the finish line. In other words, if a student changes their major and as a result of this change, needs to take additional courses, students may not graduate on schedule. For example, in 2011 the Institutional Research Department at Colorado State

University reported that changing a major adds about a half semester to the graduation timetable. This obviously has financial implications for students. Not only does this mean that students need to spend money on additional courses, it also extends the opportunity costs associated with attending college because students will not yet be able to benefit from the higher earnings associated with having a degree.

Perhaps a better approach would be for colleges to create first-semester schedules that are very flexible in terms of the curriculum. In other words, encourage students to take general education courses that are required of all students, regardless of major or meta-major. This way, students can use the first semester to actively engage in career exploration and not have to worry about whether courses will count toward graduation.

This approach buys the student some time to explore before having to make a decision. Meta-majors might then be introduced during the second semester to aid students still not completely sure about a specific major. Freedman (2013) argues that students should not choose a major until their second year noting that "choosing a major is a choice that should be intentional and based on knowledge of one's self, and when the wrong choice is made, the implications can be harsh" (para. 1). She advocates to use exploratory versus undecided language and believes that strong advising needs to be integrated into the first-year experience.

Striking a balance between career exploration and choosing a major has become increasingly more important for students receiving financial aid. With high percentages of students receiving financial aid, it is important to note that deciding on a major or career path is often connected to financial resources. In order to remain eligible for federal grants and loans, students must select a program and complete their program requirements within a timely fashion. Typically, financial aid is only available for courses that are a part of their curriculum. Students who change their major multiple times will find it difficult to be aligned with federal regulations related to maximum time frame, and as a result, they may lose their aid before completing their degree (Kantrowitz, 2012).

Kay McClenney coined the phrase "students don't do optional" (Fain, 2012). In this context, students are not likely to engage in career exploration unless required to do so. This is probably true for all of us. We are all very busy, juggling numerous academic, social, and personal tasks. It is no different for students. Although students may be interested in exploring career paths, priority is given to tasks that must be completed today or in the very near future. Greenbank and Hepworth (2008) refer to this as the serial approach to academics and career, focusing first on what must be done immediately. Unfortunately, this means that many college students are spending very little time, if any at all, on the career exploration process.

THE CAREER EXPLORATION AND
DECISION-MAKING PROCESS

How do students decide on a career path? According to research, students tend to rely on informal approaches. More specifically, students are most likely to find out career information from friends and family as opposed to career specialists (Greenbank & Hepworth, 2008). After receiving guidance from family and friends, students do not spend much time researching career options (Beggs et al., 2008).

While an informal approach can work for some students, it is not ideal. This reliance on family and friends is more advantageous to students who come from privileged backgrounds because their family and friend network will often possess a wealth of information about many different prestigious careers. On the other hand, students who do not come from privileged backgrounds may only have access to limited information about a few career options. Thus, this informal approach to career exploration and decision making clearly puts students at either an advantage or a disadvantage and as a result, can contribute to the academic achievement gap. Colleges that want to effectively meet the needs of all their students and close the academic achievement gaps will therefore not want to leave career exploration to chance.

When students do seek out career guidance at the college level, they are more likely to talk with their professors as opposed to meeting with a trained career counselor (Greenbank & Hepworth, 2008). This is because students often develop a relationship with their professors over the course of a semester and because it is more convenient to speak with a professor before or after class as opposed to scheduling an appointment with a career counselor.

Talking with a faculty member about career options can be quite beneficial for two reasons. First, the professor has expertise in the discipline so will therefore likely know a lot about career options in that field. Second, the professor has hopefully learned about the student's interests, abilities, and values over the course of the semester, and as a result, the conversation about careers can be easily personalized.

However, faculty are not necessarily trained on how to best assist students with engaging in the career exploration process. Career exploration is not typically a part of their discipline expertise and most faculty development focuses on teaching rather than advising responsibilities. When faculty are provided with professional development opportunities in the area of advising, it is often very technical in nature. For instance, advising training often focuses on how to use technology tools. Faculty may not be aware of strategies or tools available to assist students with gaining self-awareness or accessing career information. Given their many other responsibilities, faculty may also not be able to devote much time to learning how to engage students in conversations about career exploration. Likewise, faculty may not have the time to devote to providing in-depth career guidance to students.

Career counselors, on the other hand, have professional training on how to engage students in career decision making. In other words, career counselors have the knowledge, skills, and resources to help students explore options and make career decisions. In addition, this is the primary task of career counselors, so they have the time needed to support students. Yet, many students do not take advantage of this resource.

In fact, in a study conducted by Vertsberger and Gati (2015), it was found that only 8% of the students in the study met with a career advisor even though there was no cost for this benefit. Thus, it doesn't really matter how wonderful and amazing the services are if students are not taking advantage of them. Optional supports may also promote the equity gap as higher performing students and students from more privileged backgrounds are more likely to know the value of networking and professional services and therefore will be more likely to take advantage of and use career counseling services. Thus, using a required course such as the first-year seminar to provide all students with support related to career exploration is advisable.

Decision making is an important skill and making a decision about a career path is one of the most important decisions facing college students. Unfortunately, students often make career decisions without fully engaging in the decision-making process. Crittenden and Woodside (2007) note that many decisions are made with very limited information or data. Students are more likely to make a good choice when they engage in the following six steps of decision making: (1) determine your goal(s) and have your goal(s) guide the decision-making process; (2) obtain the information needed to make an informed decision; (3) identify possible options; (4) evaluate the pros and cons of each option identified; (5) take action and make a decision; and (6) assess or evaluate whether or not the decision was good one and select a different option if needed (Harrington, 2019).

Goal Setting

Before turning our attention to career decision making specifically, it is important to understand goal setting in general. Despite research that shows a strong relationship between setting effective goals and achieving at higher levels, many students have not learned how to set effective goals (Moeller, Theiler, & Wu, 2012). In fact, in a 2009 study conducted by Bishop and cited in Moeller et al. (2012), 85% of students reported that they did not learn how to set goals.

Perhaps the most well-known goal-setting framework is SMART goals; this framework is frequently used in many different fields such as academia and business. The SMART goal approach focuses on setting goals that are

Specific, Measurable, Achievable, Realistic or relevant, and Time-based. Although the SMART goal framework is widely used, Day and Tosey (2011) note that the data on the effectiveness of this approach are quite limited.

Some components of this approach have strong research support. For example, research has consistently demonstrated the value of goals being specific and measurable (Locke and Latham, 2002). However, other components of the SMART framework have less or even inconsistent data. In particular, the research on whether or not goals need to be realistic is mixed. Some researchers have found that it is important to set realistic goals because setting unrealistic goals may result in poorer performance (Brusso, Orvis, Bauer, & Tekleab, 2012), but other researchers have not been able to find any negative consequence of setting unrealistic goals (Linde, Jeffrey, Finch, Ng, & Rothman, 2004).

Perhaps the greatest concern with the SMART framework is the absence of challenge as a goal characteristic, which has been consistently found to be an essential part of the goal-setting process. After reviewing 35 years of goal-setting research, Locke and Latham (2002) found that challenge was an incredibly important component of effective goal setting. In fact, challenge—along with specificity—were noted to be the goal-setting characteristics with the strongest level of research support.

Given this research, a new goal-setting framework was developed by Harrington (2019). The ABCS goal-setting approach involves the following components:

- **A**im high
- **B**elieve in yourself
- **C**are and commit
- **S**pecify and self-reflect

First and foremost, this framework focuses on the importance of setting challenging goals and aiming high. Research has shown that we are not very likely to achieve at a level higher than our goals. For example, Reynolds and Baird (2010) conducted a fascinating study where they asked high school students to share their educational attainment goal (i.e., high school, associate's degree, bachelor's degree, graduate degree) and then tracked these students to find out if they achieved the goal they set out to achieve as a high school student.

Results indicated that only 8% of participants achieved at a level higher than their stated goal in high school, while almost half (49%) achieved their goal and 43% fell short of achieving their goal. Interestingly, this research also illustrated resiliency. Specifically, Reynolds and Baird (2010) found that there was no emotional cost for unrealized goals. In other words, the level of depressive symptoms was not higher for those who did not achieve their goal as compared to those who did achieve their goal.

In addition to emphasizing the importance of setting high goals, this ABCS goal-setting framework also focuses on self-efficacy (believe in yourself) and motivation (care and commit). According to Bandura (1997), self-efficacy refers to one's belief in their ability to successfully complete a task or achieve a goal. Self-efficacy related to career decision making can impact the decisions that are made. For example, a student who believes they will be able to successfully explore options and decide on a career path will be more likely to actively engage in the career exploration process. On the other hand, a student with low self-efficacy in career decision making may instead avoid tasks related to career exploration. It is therefore important that self-efficacy be considered during the career exploration process.

In addition, students with higher levels of motivation are also more likely to take actions needed to make an informed decision about which career path is best. When we care about something, we are more likely to invest in the process even if the tasks are time-consuming or difficult. Likewise, we are more likely to persist with a task, even after becoming frustrated or encountering roadblocks, when we have committed to the goal (Turner and Husman, 2008). Frustration is likely as students strive to determine the best career path as there are literally thousands of career options to consider. Thus, helping students commit to this process at the start is important.

Finally, the ABCS goal-setting framework also focuses on the importance of developing goals that are specific and then engaging in self-reflective practices to monitor progress toward the achievement of these goals. Locke and Latham (2006) found very strong research evidence for creating specific goals, noting that specific goals led to the best outcomes. This is probably, in part, because specific goals enable the person to easily monitor progress. In other words, when a goal is very specific, it is easy to determine if the goal has been achieved or whether or not one is on track to achieve the goal. Monitoring progress toward goals is essential. In fact, researchers have found that students who regularly engage in self-reflective practices and monitor their progress are more likely to meet with success (Schloemer & Brenan, 2006; Zimmerman, 2002).

Helping students use a research-based framework such as the ABCS goal-setting framework will lead to positive outcomes. Research has found that students who learn how to set effective goals achieve at higher levels as compared to students who do not learn how to set effective goals (Morisano, Hirsch, Peterson, Pihl, & Shore, 2010). Knowing how to set goals effectively will be helpful to students faced with career exploration and decision making. It is therefore essential that goal setting be incorporated into career exploration and decision-making processes.

Career Theories

There are a variety of theories related to careers that can be used to guide the career exploration and decision-making process. We will briefly describe the five following career theories, focusing on how these theories can guide the career exploration process:

- Frank Parsons's Trait and Factor Theory
- John Holland's Person-Environment Fit Theory
- Donald Super's Developmental Theory
- John Krumboltz's Happenstance Theory
- Albert Bandura's Social Cognitive Theory

Before we dive into career theories that can be beneficial in helping students choose a pathway, it is important to note that the end goal can be choosing a career *pathway* rather than a specific career. Although some students may decide on a very specific career and this specificity can help students select courses and experiences aligned to this goal, choosing a very specific career is not necessary during the first semester for two reasons.

First, most college or university curricula have many shared courses across majors that are similar in nature. For example, students in accounting and management majors will both probably need to take similar math and business courses. Likewise, the health fields will likely require similar foundational courses in the sciences. Therefore a meta-major or career pathway approach can be helpful; the shared courses are highlighted for students.

Second, most of us will likely have numerous career experiences throughout our lifetime. In fact, the average person is likely to have 11.7 different jobs over the course of their lifetime (United States Department of Labor, Bureau of Labor Statistics, 2017). Unfortunately, there is no data to inform us about how many of these job changes are career changes, switching from one field to another. The Bureau of Labor Statistics (United States Department of Labor, n.d.) notes that the lack of data available to answer this question is because "no consensus has emerged on what constitutes a career change." Because we are likely to change positions, and many of these positions may not even exist today, it may not be that important for students to choose a specific career. However, identifying a career pathway will make educational planning a much easier process.

Frank Parsons's Trait and Factor Theory

Parsons is often viewed as the founder of the vocational guidance movement. In 1909, Parsons developed the first trait and factor approach to career exploration and decision making. He believed that matching individual traits such as interests and abilities to the jobs available in the job market was the best way to approach career decision making. According to Parsons (1909), there are three main steps to deciding on a career: (1) self-awareness of individual interests and abilities, (2) learning about the job market and what jobs exist, and (3) making a career decision that aligns individual traits with the job market data. This approach is still widely used today.

John Holland's Person-Environment Fit Theory

Holland's (1997) approach is perhaps one of the most commonly used approaches to career exploration and decision making today. It expands on the work of Parsons (1909), with a more comprehensive look at individual interests and personality traits as well as work environments. Holland (1997) believes that career decisions should be made by looking for work environments that match individual interests and personality. Holland (1997) identified the following six themes that characterize both the individual and the work environment:

1. Realistic (working with things and/or outdoors)
2. Investigative (working with ideas)
3. Artistic (using creativity; working independently)
4. Social (working with others)
5. Enterprising (influencing or persuading others)
6. Conventional (working on structured tasks; detail-oriented)

Holland believed that the more congruence there was between a person and their work environment, the more satisfied one would be. According to this theory, matching the person's interests to the tasks of the work environment is at the crux of career decision making. This theoretical approach has been strongly supported by research (Jagger, Neukrug, & McAuliffe, 1992; Nauta, 2010).

In a large, longitudinal study with over 80,000 students from 87 colleges, it was found that students with higher levels of congruence between their interests and major were more likely to perform better academically, as measured by grade point average (Tracey & Robbins, 2006). Similarly, research has found that interest-major congruence has been found to be associated with graduating on schedule. Allen and Robbins (2010), for instance, found that "higher levels of interest-major congruence lead to greater likelihood of attaining a degree in a timely fashion" (p. 32).

There are numerous assessment tools available to assist students with determining which of the six themes best characterizes their interests and personality. After completing assessments such as the Self-Directed Search, students will walk away with a three-letter code that captures their top three interest areas in order of importance. To assist students with matching or aligning their preferences to the world of work, careers have been cataloged with three-letter codes. Websites such as ONET (www.onetonline.org) use Holland's themes to organize career options. This way, students can search careers by their preferred code. For example, a student with a realistic, investigative, and conventional (RIC) code can easily see many career choices such as logistics engineer, web developer, and chemist that match their interests in these areas.

Donald Super's Developmental Theory

Super's contribution to the field of career exploration and decision making focused primarily on his life-span, developmental approach. Super recognized that people have multiple roles in work and in their personal life and that the nature of these roles and the demands associated with each one vary based on stages of development (Herr, 1997). More specifically, Super identified the following five stages in the career life cycle:

1. Growth—development of self-concept and understanding of the world of work
2. Exploration—exploring vocational options
3. Establishment—skill development and initial achievements
4. Maintenance—making adjustments as needed
5. Decline—planning for retirement

According to Super's developmental theory, self-concept plays a central role in career development. Careers that build self-efficacy and develop self-concept are what lead to high levels of satisfaction. Researchers have found support for this stages approach to understanding career development (Smart & Peterson, 1994).

Krumboltz's Happenstance Theory

Krumboltz (2009) is a social learning psychologist who focused on a concept he calls happenstance. After listening to many different individuals describe their career paths, Krumboltz and Levin (2004) discovered that most of us are not following a planned, predictable path to our career. Instead, he found that career decisions are made based on a series of planned and unplanned events. Although Krumboltz (2009) acknowledges the importance of self-awareness, he believes that what is most important is being open to experiences and taking actions that may lead to new opportunities.

According to happenstance theory, students need to seek out new opportunities and frequently talk with others about their career-related ideas and aspirations. For example, it is important to encourage students to take advantage of internships, volunteer experiences, and to take active steps such as conducting informational interviews to learn more about various career options. It is often through these social experiences and connections that a student decides on a career path.

Albert Bandura's Social Cognitive Theory

According to the social cognitive theory of career, social or situational factors play an essential role in career decision making (Lent, Brown, & Hackett, 1994). One example is how our loved ones can influence our career decisions. Phillips, Christopher-Sisk, and Gravino (2001) note that our friends and family often make suggestions about careers or make connections to help us explore options and gain valuable working experience. Another way that our social world influences our career decisions is through role models. We learn about different careers through personal role models in the community (Nauta & Kokaly, 2001).

In addition to social or situational factors impacting our career decisions, cognition also plays an important role. More specifically, self-efficacy influences the career decision making process (Lent et al., 1994). A student who believes they will be successful in a career is more likely to further explore that career option. Conversely, if a student has low self-efficacy, few options may be considered or explored. Self-efficacy is higher if we have experienced success previously, so our past experiences play an important role in our decision making about the future.

Exploratory Actions

There are several ways that students can put career theories into practice and take action. First, it is important to recognize that this process is complex and takes time. Increasing self-awareness, knowledge about career options, and career skills such as networking are all important. Assisting students with actively engaging in the career exploration process will help them make more informed and better choices about a career path.

Self-exploration related to careers typically begins by considering interests. As just discussed, interests are a key component of several theories, especially Parsons's and Holland's theories. Students are often able to easily identify what they like and dislike. There are, of course, several assessment tools available that can assist students with thinking about their interests, as well as their abilities, values, and personality factors. However, the career exploration process must go beyond having students complete a career inventory.

Behrens and Nauta (2014) compared students who completed the Self-Directed Search, an assessment tool aligned to Holland's theory, to students who did not complete the inventory. Although the students who completed the inventory were able to identify more career options or alternatives, there were no differences between the groups on career exploration activities, decision-making self-efficacy, seeking career counseling, or making career decisions. In 2003, Karp (cited in Bailey et al., 2015) also noted that there is no connection between completing an inventory and earning a credential, meaning that students who complete self-assessment inventories do not seem to get to the finish line more than students who do not complete these inventories.

Knowing abilities, values, and personality factors can also prove useful in the career decision making process. As students strive to increase their self-awareness, it is therefore important for these factors to be a part of the process. For example, students can evaluate their strengths or abilities based on their prior experiences such as academic coursework or other experiences. Encouraging students to think about technical and soft skills is important. Technical skills are more specific to career fields while soft skills are skills such as communication and interpersonal skills that are useful in many, if not all, careers (Robles, 2012).

In addition to developing technical and soft skills, students will want to develop skills related to career exploration. Networking, for example, is one of the most important skills needed when it comes to career success (DeVos, DeClippeleer, & Dewilde, 2009). More specifically, individuals who are effective at networking are more likely to be employed and be satisfied with their career (Van Hoye, van Hooft, & Lievens, 2009; Wolff & Moser, 2009; Villar, Juan, Corominas, & Capell, 2000). It is therefore important for students to learn how to make connections with professionals and to grow and foster these relationships.

Values are incredibly important in the career exploration process. Students will want to seek out career opportunities that align with their values or what matters to them. Choi et al. (2013) identified several work values such as helping others, independence, leadership, responsibility, high income, job security, prestige, and easy access to the job. When values clash with the career, dissatisfaction is very likely. It is therefore critical for students to spend time thinking about what truly matters to them now and what might be of importance to them in the future. Balsamo, Lauriola and Saggino (2013) note that values play an essential role in decision making.

Personality can also impact career decision making. The Myers Briggs personality assessment is often used to assist individuals with career decision making. Hirsh and Kummerow (cited in Kennedy & Kennedy, 2004) identify four primary personality factors in this assessment. The first is extroversion or introversion and focuses on whether individuals get energy from others (extroversion) or from within (introversion). The second factor is sensing and intuition. Those who prefer to pay attention to what can be seen are high on sensing while those who prefer to think about what might be are more likely to be high on intuition. Thinking and feeling is the next dimension and focuses on whether individuals prefer to approach information from a logical perspective (thinking) or based on personal values and emotions (feeling). Finally, individuals can prefer planning and organization (judgment) or being spontaneous and flexible (perceiving). The more students know about themselves, the more likely it is that they will choose a career path that matches their interests, values, and abilities. Advisors or counselors can help students engage in the self-assessment process by asking relevant questions. While assessment tools can be used for this purpose, it can often be just as effective to engage in a conversation where students are asked questions about their interests, values, and abilities.

Researching careers is the next step in the process. There are several strategies that students can use to find out about various career options. One strategy is to use career information websites such as the Occupational Outlook Handbook or ONET. These websites provide an overview of most careers. For example, students will learn about the job duties, educational requirements, salary, and job outlook. Another strategy is to talk with individuals about their experience in their position. This can happen through informal conversations or through a more formal approach such as the informational interview. Crosby (2010) notes that the goal of the informational interview is an opportunity to meet with a professional in the field and learn about the career. Job shadowing is another excellent approach. Job shadowing involves watching a professional in a field of interest perform their daily tasks.

It is important to note that as many theories suggest, gathering information about oneself and the world of work may not be enough to assist students with making career decisions. In many cases, experiential opportunities are critical to this process. Students with varied experiences will find it easier to engage in the self-assessment process. The more experiences students have, the more data they have to reflect on as they consider their interests, abilities, and values. Krumboltz (2009), for instance, focuses on the critical role of experiential learning opportunities such as volunteering or internships. Thus, one of the most effective career decision-making strategies may be to get students involved in college and in the wider community. These experiences will without a doubt prove useful to students during the career decision-making process.

BENEFITS OF CAREER EXPLORATION VIA THE FIRST-YEAR SEMINAR COURSE

Mandatory career exploration is needed. Requiring career exploration of all students sends a very powerful message about the importance of these actions. It is also a way to address equity issues; requiring all students to engage in career-related actions ensures that all students will benefit from the experience. As previously discussed, voluntary programs are more likely to be utilized by students of more privileged backgrounds because they are more likely to realize the value of these services.

The biggest challenge associated with mandating advising or career exploration is limited resources. Colleges do not typically have the resources to require students to see an advisor. In some colleges, the caseload of an advisor can be 1,000 students or more. This makes it next to impossible for the advisor to really get to know each student. In addition, there simply are not enough hours in the day for advisors to be able to have multiple meetings with students. Career exploration requires more than a few conversations with a career expert. Leveraging a current resource such as the first-year seminar, particularly if this course is required by all students, is a great way to maximize current resources to better meet the needs of students.

The most important benefit of requiring career exploration via the first-year seminar is that this approach makes it more likely that students will engage in career exploration. As Greenbank and Hepworth (2008) noted, students are more likely to focus on assignments as opposed to other activities that are not "due" soon. Thus, the class approach adds credibility to the tasks and serves as a motivator for students to take actions related to career decision making.

In addition, it gives students the opportunity to deeply engage in this process over the course of an entire semester. Through carefully crafted assignments, students can increase their self-awareness of interests, skills, and values as well as develop skills, such as networking, that are essential to career success. First-year seminars that focus on career exploration throughout the entire semester, rather than having just one or two isolated lessons on this topic, will be more likely to result in more positive outcomes. This in-depth approach is what is needed to truly assist students with making good decisions about careers. Many of the core academic skills that are often a focus of the first-year seminar course can also be taught using a career focus. For example, information literacy, reading, and note-taking can be taught as students engage in a career project.

Some colleges have incorporated the first-year seminar into the meta-major or career pathway approach, meaning that special sections of the course are offered for each meta-major or career pathway. In other words, there could be different sections for students in the business field versus health or the liberal arts. One advantage of this approach is that the examples and career exploration could be focused within that particular career path. This can be especially helpful for students who are clear about their pathway but not certain about the specific career.

When colleges use this approach, faculty and student engagement can be higher because there is a shared interest in the field. The disadvantage, of course, is that the information will likely be limited to that specific career path and thus the content may not be as relevant if a student changes his or her major. In most cases, the learning outcomes for first-year seminars for different pathways will likely be the same. For example, engaging students in career exploration and building information literacy and critical thinking skills would likely be learning outcomes for all first-year seminar courses, regardless of their meta-major or discipline focus. In this situation, the curriculum would therefore be more similar than different across different career pathways. Based on this perspective, the meta-major or career pathway discipline-specific approach may not be necessary, especially if it poses many logistical issues related to delivery and implementation. Colleges can find it very challenging to offer all versions of the first-year seminar on all campuses and at all different times of the day or evening. In addition, it can be challenging to find faculty from each discipline to teach the course.

Learning from peers is another advantage of using the first-year seminar course to assist students with engaging in career exploration and decision making. In addition to learning from their own research and self-exploration, students can gather information about careers from a variety of sources and learn from the experiences of their classmates. This will be particularly true if students are required to share what they have learned via presentations, as presentations can serve as another avenue for students to learn about different careers. It is very possible that a student may have never considered a career until they hear their classmate provide an overview of the career during a presentation. In essence, the course can be used as a way to increase exposure to options that a student may not have even known about prior to the class. While this can happen in meta-major versions of the first-year seminar, a wider exposure to various career options is more likely in a first-year seminar that is more general in nature.

Another benefit of using first-year seminars as a vehicle to assist students with career exploration is that it builds on student-professor relationships that already exist. As previously discussed, students are more likely to seek career guidance from faculty as opposed to career counselors (Greenbank & Hepworth, 2008). This is because students develop relationships with their professors over the course of the semester. It is even more likely for first-year seminar instructors to have strong relationships with their students, given the personal nature of the course. Thus, instructors of first-year seminar courses are well-positioned to assist students with the career exploration and decision-making process.

Although not all first-year seminar instructors will be experts on assisting students with career decision making, training on how to best assist students with making career choices can be provided. The expertise of career counselors can be utilized to develop a training program for instructors. Career counselors or advisors may also want to serve as liaisons for classes, perhaps even meeting with the students a couple of times during the semester. With training, first-year seminar instructors will have increased confidence when assisting students with career decision making.

In summary, the career exploration process is complex and time-consuming, and there are various career theories that guide our work. The career exploration process involves engaging in self-assessment, exploring career options, and taking advantage of experiential learning opportunities. Requiring in-depth career exploration in the first-year seminar is an excellent way to increase the likelihood that students will be engaged in this process. As a result, students will be more likely to make meaningful career decisions.

REFERENCES

Albion, M. J., & Fogarty, G. J. (2002). Factors influencing career decision making in adolescents and adults. *Journal of Career Assessment, 10*(1), 91–126.

Allen, J., & Robbins, S. (2010). Effects of interest-major congruence, motivation, and academic performance on timely degree attainment. *Journal of Counseling Psychology, 57*(10), 23–35.

Bailey, T. R., Smith Jaggars, S., & Jenkins, D. (2015). *Redesigning America's community colleges: A clearer path to student success.* Cambridge, MA: Harvard University Press.

Balsamo, M., Lauriola, M., & Saggino, A. (2013). Work values and college major choice. *Learning and Individual Differences, 24*, 110–116.

Bandura, A. (1997). *Self-efficacy: The exercise of control.* New York: Freeman.

Beggs, J. M., Bantham, J. H., & Taylor, S. (2008). Distinguishing the factors influencing college students' choice of major. *College Student Journal, 42*(2), 381–394.

Behrens, E. L., & Nauta, M. M. (2014). The self-directed search as a stand-alone intervention with college students. *The Career Development Quarterly, 62*(3), 224–238. doi:10.1002/j.2161-0045.2014.00081.x

Brusso, R. C., Orvis, K. A., Bauer, K. N., & Tekleab, A. G. (2012). Interaction among self-efficacy, goal orientation, and unrealistic goal-setting on videogame-based training performance. *Military Psychology, 24*(1), 1–18.

Choi, B. Y., Kim, B., Jang, S. H., Jung, S. H., Ahn, S. S., Lee, S. M., & Gysbers, N. (2013). An individual's work values in career development. *Journal of Employment Counseling, 50*(4), 154–165. doi:10.1002/j.2161-1920.2013.00034.x

Colorado State University (2011). Major changes and persistence patterns. *Institutional Research, Planning and Effectiveness Research Briefs.* Retrieved from: http://www.ir.colostate.edu/research-brief-categories/

Crittenden, V., & Woodside, A. G. (2007). Building skills in thinking: Toward a pedagogy in metathinking. *Journal of Education for Business*, 37–44.

Crosby, O. (2010, Summer). Informational interviewing: Get the inside scoop on careers. *Occupational Outlook Quarterly, 54*(2), 22–29.

Cuseo, J. (n.d.) Requiring early (premature?) decisions about a college major: Some considerations. Unpublished manuscript.

Day, T., & Tosey, P. (2011). Beyond SMART? A new framework for goal setting. *Curriculum Journal, 22*(4), 515–534.

DeVos, A., DeClippeleer, I., & Dewilde, T. (2009). Proactive career behaviours and career success during the early career. *Journal of Occupational and Organizational Psychology, 82*, 761–777.

Drysdale, M. T. B., Frost, N., & McBeath, M. L. (2015). How often do they change their minds and does work-integrated learning play a role? An examination of "major changes" and career certainty in higher education. *Asia-Pacific Journal of Cooperative Education, 16*(2), 145–152.

Fain, P. (2012). Make it mandatory? *Inside Higher Ed.* Retrieved from https://www.insidehighered.com/news/2012/02/02/academic-support-offerings-go-unused-community-colleges

Freedman, L. (2013). The developmental disconnect in choosing a major: Why institutions should prohibit choice until second year. *The Mentor, an Academic Advising Journal,* Penn State Division of Undergraduate Studies. Retrieved from https://dus.psu.edu/mentor/2013/06/disconnect-choosing-major/

Gati, I., Krausz, M., & Osipow, S. H. (1996). A taxonomy of difficulties in career decision making. *Journal of Counseling Psychology, 43*(4), 510–526.

Greenbank, P., & Hepworth, S. (2008). Working-class students and the career decision-making process: A qualitative study, HECSU, Manchester, available at http://www.hecsu.ac.uk/assets/assets/documents/Working_class.pdf. Accessed March 3, 2016.

Harrington, C. (2019). *Student success in college: Doing what works!* 3rd edition. Boston: MA: Cengage Learning.

Herr, E. L. (1997). Super's life-span, life-space approach and its outlook for refinement. *The Career Development Quarterly, 45*(3), 238–246. doi:10.1002/j.2161-0045.1997.tb00468.x

Holland, J. L. (1997). *Making vocational choices: Theory of vocational personalities and work environments.* Odessa, FL: Psychological Assessment Resources.

Iyengar, S. S., & Lepper, M. R. (2000). When choice is demotivating: Can one desire too much of a good thing? *Journal of Personality and Social Psychology, 79*(6), 995–1006. doi:10.1037/0022-3514.79.6.995

Jagger, L., Neukrug, E., & McAuliffe, G. (1992). Congruence between personality traits and chosen occupation as a predictor of job satisfaction for people with disabilities. *Rehabilitation Counseling Bulletin, 36*(1), 53–60. Retrieved from Academic Search Premiere database.

Kantrowitz, M. (2012). *Can a student be cut off from financial aid after taking too many credits?* Retrieved from Fastweb website: https://www.fastweb.com/financial-aid/articles/can-a-student-be-cut-off-from-financial-aid-after-taking-too-many-credits

Kennedy, R. B., & Kennedy, D. A. (2004). Using the Myers-Briggs type indicator in career counseling. *Journal of Employment Counseling, 41*(1), 38–44.

Krumboltz, J. D. (2009). The happenstance learning theory. *Journal of Career Assessment, 17*(2), 135–154.

Krumboltz, J., & Levin, A. (2004). *Luck is no accident: Making the most of happenstance in your life and career.* Atascadero, CA: Impact.

Latham, G. P., & Locke, E. A. (2006). Enhancing the benefits and overcoming the pitfalls of goal setting. *Organizational Dynamics, 35*(4), 332–340. doi:10.1016/j.orgdyn.2006.08.008.

Lent, R. W., Brown, S. D., & Hackett, G. (1994). Toward a unifying social cognitive theory of career and academic interest, choice, and performance. *Journal of Vocational Behavior, 45,* 79–122.

Linde, J. A., Jeffrey, R. W., Finch, E. A., Ng, D. M., & Rothman, A. J. (2004). Are unrealistic weight loss goals associated with outcomes for overweight women? *Obesity Research, 12*(2), 569–576.

Locke, E. A., & Latham, G. P. (2002). Building a practically useful theory of goal setting and task motivation: A 35-year odyssey. *American Psychologist, 57*(9), 705–717. doi:10.1037/0003066X.57.9.705

Micceri, T. (2001). Change your major and double your graduation chances. Paper presented at the AIR Forum 2001, Long Beach, CA, 1–9. Retrieved from ERIC database. ED 4553 756.

Moeller, A. J., Theiler, J. M., & Wu, C. (2012). Goal setting and student achievement: A longitudinal study. *Modern Language Journal, 96*(2), 153–169. Retrieved from Academic Search Premiere.

Morisano, D., Hirsh, J. B., Peterson, J. B., Pihl, R. O., & Shore, B. M. (2010). Setting, elaborating, and reflecting on personal goals improves academic performance. *Journal of Applied Psychology, 95*(2), 255–264. doi:10.1037/a0018478

National Center for Education Statistics (2017). *The condition of education 2017: Sources of financial aid.* Retrieved from https://nces.ed.gov/programs/coe/indicator_cuc.asp

Nauta, M. M. (2010). The development, evolution, and status of Holland's theory of vocational personalities: Reflections and future directions for counseling psychology. *Journal of Counseling Psychology, 57*(1), 11–22. doi:10.1037/a0018213

Nauta, M. M., & Kokaly, M. L. (2001). Assessing role model influences on students' academic and vocational decisions. *Journal of Career Assessment, 9*(1), 81-99.

Parsons, F. (1909). *Choosing a vocation.* Boston: Houghton Mifflin.

Phillips, S. D., Christopher-Sisk, E. K., & Gravino, K. L. (2001). Making career decisions in a relational context. *The Counseling Psychologist, 29*(2), 193–213.

Rebles, M. M. (2012, December). Executive perceptions of the top 10 soft skills needed in today's workplace. *Business Communication Quarterly, 75*(4), 453–465.

Reynolds, J. R., & Baird, C. L. (2010). Is there a downside to shooting for the stars? Unrealized educational expectations and symptoms of depression. *American Sociological Review, 75*(1), 151–172

Schloemer, P., & Brenan, K. (2006). From students to learners: Developing self-regulated learning. *Journal of Education for Business, 82*(2), 81–87.

Smart, R. M., & Peterson, C. C. (1994). Super's stages and the four-factor structure of the Adult Career Concerns Inventory in an Australian sample. *Measurement and Evaluation in Counseling and Development, 26*(4), 243–257.

Taveira, M. C., & Moreno, M. R. (2003). Guidance theory and practice: The status of career exploration. *British Journal of Guidance & Counselling, 31*(2), 189–207. doi:10.1080/0306988031000102360

Tracey, T. J. G., & Robbins, S. B. (2006). The interest-major congruence and college success relation: A longitudinal study. *Journal of Vocational Behavior, 69*, 64–89.

Turner, J. E., & Husman, J. (2008). Emotional and cognitive self-regulation following academic shame. *Journal of Advanced Academics, 20*(1), 138–173.

United States Department of Labor, Bureau of Labor Statistics (2017). Number of jobs, labor market experience, and earnings growth among Americans at 50: Results from a longitudinal study. Retrieved from https://www.bls.gov/news.release/nlsoy.toc.htm

United States Department of Labor, Bureau of Statistics (n.d.). National longitudinal studies. Retrieved from https://www.bls.gov/nls/nlsfaqs.htm#anch43

Van Hoye, G., van Hooft, E. A. J., & Lievens, F. (2009). Networking as a job search behavior: A social network perspective. *Journal of Occupational and Organizational Psychology, 82*, 661–682. doi: 10.1348/096317908X360675

Vertsberger, D., & Gati, I. (2015). The effectiveness of sources of support in career decision making: A two-year follow up. *Journal of Vocational Behavior, 89*, 151–161. doi: 10.1016/j.jvb.2015.06.004

Villar, E., Juan, J., Corominas, E., & Capell, D. (2000). What kind of networking strategy advice should career counsellors offer university graduates searching for a job? *British Journal of Guidance and Counselling, 28*(3), 389–409.

Wolff, H., & Moser, K. (2009). Effects of networking on career success: A longitudinal study. *Journal of Applied Psychology, 94*(1), 196–206.

Zimmerman, B. J. (2002). Becoming a self-regulated learner: An overview. *Theory Into Practice, 41*(2), 64–72. Retrieved from ERIC database.

Chapter Four

Helping Students Stay on the Path

The Role of the First-Year Seminar Course

Colleges and universities have long been invested in assisting students with meeting with success and graduating. Unfortunately, too many students are not achieving their goals and are leaving college without a credential or degree. In fact, national graduation rates leave much to be desired.

According to the U.S. Department of Education, National Center for Education Statistics (2017), the average graduation rate for first-time, full-time students entering a bachelor's degree program and completing it within 6 years is 59% and the average graduation rate for first-time, full-time students seeking a certificate or an associate's degree and completing it within 3 years is 29%. The Guided Pathways movement has been developed to address this issue and improve successful outcomes for students (Bailey, Smith Jaggars, & Jenkins, 2015).

A critical component of Guided Pathways is helping students stay on their chosen path. Although colleges and universities have always provided students with numerous resources such as advising and tutoring to help students meet with success, support services are almost always optional and therefore do not typically reach all students. Advising is a great example. Advisors can support students throughout their college journey, helping to keep students on their chosen path. However, most colleges and universities do not require students to meet with their advisor and when they do, the conversation is often focused on registration issues rather than helping students monitor their progress toward their goals and engage in actions that will lead to success.

In a national survey conducted by the National Academic Advising Association (2011), only 36.5% of higher education institutions responding to the survey indicated that advising was mandatory for all students. Advising is not the only student service that is optional and underutilized. Vertsberger and Gati (2015) found that only 8% of students responding to a survey indicated visiting with a career services professional. Thus, many students are not taking advantage of support services.

Having an optional approach to advising or other support services is particularly problematic from an equity perspective. This optional approach can widen rather than narrow achievement gaps since many of the students who need the support the most are ones who are least likely to seek it out. Schwitzer (2005), for instance, found that students who were considered low risk were the most likely to seek out counseling services. Brownson et al. (2014) reported that help-seeking behavior varies across racial and ethnic groups, with students of color reporting lower rates of help-seeking despite higher levels of distress. It is therefore critical that colleges and universities find ways to assist students who may need the services the most.

When students do take advantage of support services offered by colleges, success is more likely. For example, research has found that students who participated in tutoring were more likely to have higher levels of academic performance (Grillo & Leist, 2013). Similarly, students who met with their advisor were more likely to stay in school (Ryan, 2013). Thus, support services can assist students with staying on the path and completing their goals.

To assist all students with getting to the finish line and graduating with the skills and experiences needed to be successful in graduate school or the world of work, colleges and universities need to move beyond offering support services and toward designing support services that reach all students. Karp and Stacey (2013) note that "It is clear that support activities need to be integrated more thoroughly and consistently across the student experience" (p. 3) and advocate for colleges and universities to develop a student support approach characterized by what they call the SSIPP model. According to the SSIPP model, support services need to be sustained, strategic, integrated, proactive, and personalized.

Colleges and universities across the nation are grappling with how to redesign advising and student support services to align with the SSIPP model. Requiring students to use support services seems like an easy solution; however, this approach, while commendable, is also fraught with challenges. For starters, colleges and universities probably do not have enough staff and resources to serve all students. Advising caseloads can be up to 1,000–2,000:1 (National Academic Advising Association, 2011). Many student services professional staff are already stretched to capacity despite serving only a small subset of the student population. Given that many colleges and universities are not financially positioned to hire enough additional staff to serve all students, colleges and universities need to look to leverage current resources.

One resource that most colleges already have in place is the first-year seminar or student success course. According to a national survey, approximately 90% of colleges and universities indicated that they offer a first-year seminar course (Young & Hopp, 2014). In addition to helping students choose a path, students taking a well-designed first-year seminar can also develop strategies and skills needed to stay on their chosen path and achieve their goals. The first-year seminar course can help students stay on their path in two significant ways: (1) helping students build self-efficacy by using effective learning strategies and (2) increasing grit and resilience by engaging in productive thoughts and actions.

Helping students build self-efficacy through learning strategies is critical as academic reasons are often the most cited for students dropping out. For example, in a large-scale study of over 54,000 two- and four-year college students, students with low academic preparation were three times more likely to drop out (Mabel & Britton, 2018). In this same study, it was also found that students who passed initial courses in their program of study and introductory upper-level courses were more likely to persist and graduate. It is therefore essential that students are provided with strong support related to academic performance beginning in the first semester.

Although it is not reasonable to assume that the first-year seminar is the entire solution to poor academic preparation, this course can be a critical component of an institutional intervention. Curriculum aimed at assisting students with developing effective learning strategies will assist students with meeting the academic challenges of college. In fact, researchers have found that first-year seminars with a learning focus led to the best outcomes (Ryan & Glenn, 2004).

The first-year seminar can without a doubt help set the stage for success, helping students stay on their chosen path. "Correlational studies controlling for observable student characteristics have found evidence of short- and long-term benefits for students who enroll in student success courses, including improved academic performance, greater persistence, and increased rates of completion and transfer" (Karp & Stacey, 2013, p. 3). However, Karp and Stacey (2013) note that the benefits of the course may only last for a few semesters. Thus, it is important for student success interventions to be ongoing and integrated into the entire college experience.

BUILDING SELF-EFFICACY BY UTILIZING EFFECTIVE LEARNING AND STUDY STRATEGIES

Self-efficacy refers to one's belief about their ability to successfully complete a task. Self-efficacy will vary for different tasks. For example, a student may have high self-efficacy for math-related tasks but low or moderate self-efficacy for public speaking. Students who have high efficacy for a task are more likely to set higher goals, put forth more effort, and continue to persist when faced with challenges or obstacles (Bandura, 1977). Self-efficacy has been found to be one of the best predictors of success (Lynch, 2006). In fact, Krumrei, Newton, Kim, and Wilcox (2013) found that academic self-efficacy was a predictor of first-year grade point average, even after controlling for demographic variables and first-semester grades. Increasing academic self-efficacy can help students stay on their path.

One of the reasons why the first-year seminar is so important is that it provides students with the opportunity to establish effective learning skills at the beginning of their college journey. Engaging in effective learning approaches will increase the number of successful experiences. Successful experiences are one of the best ways to build self-efficacy (Kudo & Mori, 2015).

There is much research that shows that the academic performance during the first few weeks of the first semester is a good predictor of future success (Woosley & Miller, 2009). Other success factors, such as the amount of social support, have also been found to be very important early on. For example, DeBerard, Spielmans, and Julka (2004) found that the amount of social support during the very first week of the semester predicts success. The sooner students develop and use effective learning strategies and strengthen their strong support system, the better.

Understanding the Process of Learning

In the first-year seminar, students can establish effective learning and study practices that will serve them well throughout their college experience. Too often students are left to engage in trial-and-error approaches to studying that may not always result in positive outcomes. By incorporating research-based learning strategies into the curriculum of a course that students take their very first semester, colleges are providing high-level support to help students stay on the path and meet with success. When students use effective learning strategies, it is more likely that they will establish a deep knowledge of essential content needed for success.

Although many professionals have focused on helping students determine their individual learning styles over the past couple of decades, the body of research on learning shows that we are more similar than different in how we learn (Goswami, 2008). In fact, research has shown that there is no evidence that teaching to a student's preferred learning style has positive outcomes (Pashler, McDaniel, Rohrer, & Bjork, 2008). Instead, research shows that we are all multi-sensory learners. In other words, using several senses simultaneously will improve learning. As Brown, Roediger, and McDaniel (2014) put it, "[Y]ou learn better when you 'go wide,' drawing on all of your aptitudes and resourcefulness, than when you limit instruction or experience to the style you find most amenable" (p. 4). Thus, it is more fruitful to focus energy and time on assisting students with understanding how we all learn best rather than focusing on learning differences.

Learning begins with remembering. Having strong foundational knowledge sets the stage for higher level learning and critical thinking (Brown et al., 2014; Ozuru, Dempsey, & McNamara, 2009). The memory process involves attending to information in the environment, actively engaging with the content in working memory, and then if successful at learning the content, holding the information in long-term memory and retrieving it when needed (Willingham, 2009).

Building memories is an interactive process that is greatly impacted by prior experiences. Stanovich (2008) notes that the more you know, the easier it is for you to learn. When learning something new, we will automatically search for any prior knowledge or experience that relates or connects to the new information (Baddeley, 2002). Connecting or "sticking" new information to information that is already known increases learning. Therefore, assisting students with developing a strong knowledge base early is advantageous for students. This strong knowledge base will make it easier for students to learn new information now and in the future.

Remembering information is an important part of the learning process, but remembering is clearly not the end goal. This is why Bloom's educational taxonomy has knowledge as the first of six steps in the hierarchical process of learning (Bloom, 1956). According to Anderson and Krathwohl (2001), who revised Bloom's original taxonomy, learning involves remembering, understanding, applying, analyzing, evaluating, and creating. This is a hierarchical process whereby lower-level cognitive tasks need to happen prior to being able to successfully engage in higher-level tasks. Learning is a complex process that begins with remembering and then shifts to more and more cognitively complex tasks.

To help students stay on their path and achieve their academic goals, first-year seminar instructors can help them develop and use learning strategies that will result in a strong foundational base of knowledge. Teaching students about evidence-based study practices and finding ways to have students practice these skills in and out of the classroom will be very helpful to first-year students. After students build their general fund of knowledge, first-year instructors can begin to focus on assisting students with developing higher-level cognitive skills. Developing high-level skills, such as critical thinking, takes time and will not likely be accomplished in one semester. However, the first-year seminar can serve an important role in helping students understand the skills and strategies behind critical thinking.

First-year seminar instructors can encourage students to begin engaging in actions that facilitate critical thinking. For example, first-year seminar instructors can teach students about Bloom's (1956) taxonomy, or Harrington's process of becoming a critical thinker (Bers, Chun, Daly, Harrington, Toblowsky, & Associates, 2015). Helping students understand the cognitive processes involved in learning and thinking critically can be addressed in the first-year seminar. In addition, first-year seminar instructors can also assign challenging learning tasks that require students to apply, analyze, evaluate, and create and support students in completing these tasks.

One of the most effective techniques that can be used to foster higher-level thinking is questioning. First-year seminar instructors can, of course, ask thought-provoking questions, but this course is also a great opportunity to help students develop their own questioning skills. King (1995) is a strong advocate of teaching students how to ask good questions, believing that this is a skill that can be developed through peer reciprocal questioning. First-year seminar instructors can engage students in this process by first teaching students about the importance of questioning, providing sample question stems or model questions, and then giving students an opportunity to ask and answer questions in small and large groups. Yang, Newby, and Bill (2005), for instance, suggest teaching students about Socratic questioning, providing sample questions such as "What do you mean by ____?" "What would someone who disagrees say?" and "How did you come to believe that?" (p. 672).

Learning about learning can help students successfully achieve their goals (McGuire, 2015). The first-year seminar is a perfect opportunity to teach students about the learning process. In addition, students can practice skills that will enhance their ability to learn in and out of the first-year seminar classroom.

Discovering Evidence-Based Study Strategies

Unfortunately, students often rely on learning strategies that are only minimally effective. Dunlosky, Rawson, Marsh, Nathan, and Willingham (2013) found that students are often employing learning strategies that are of low utility. For example, one of the most widely used strategies by students is reviewing or rereading notes to study. While reviewing is an important part of the learning process, it is often not sufficient in and of itself.

Reviewing can be quite passive with students simply looking at their notes repeatedly. As a result of this process, content will seem more and more familiar and students can mistakenly interpret familiarity with learning. Reviewing often only leads to a surface-level knowledge while learning requires much deeper engagement with the content. Dunlosky et al. (2013) recommend replacing the rereading technique with other strategies that have been demonstrated to be more effective.

What learning and study approaches work best? Fortunately, researchers have thoroughly investigated this very question. Some of the most effective learning strategies include testing yourself, teaching to learn, making connections and using organizing strategies, engaging in spaced practice, and monitoring learning progress (Schwartz, Son, Kornell, & Finn, 2011; Brown et al., 2014). For a more thorough overview of learning strategies that work best, see Harrington (2019). Students who utilize these strategies regularly will develop the knowledge and skills needed to achieve their goals.

Testing Effect

One of the most powerful ways to learn is through testing, but unfortunately testing is often narrowly viewed as a way to demonstrate learning rather than as a *way to learn*. Numerous studies have shown the value of testing as a learning tool. For example, in a now classic study by Roediger and Karpicke (2006), students who had to test themselves or recall what they learned outperformed students who reviewed the content even though the students who engaged in reviewing had access to the content four times as long as the students engaged in testing. This consistent research finding has been called the testing effect, which basically means that testing is a powerful memory or learning tool. In other words, the act of retrieving content helps improve learning.

Students are more likely to use strategies if they are familiar with the strategy and see firsthand the benefits of using the approach. This was illustrated in a study that was conducted by Einstein, Mullet, and Harrison (2012). In this study, students who engaged in practice retrieval via testing and saw the improvement on test scores were more likely to report using this strategy later in the semester. Thus, it is important for students, especially first-year students, to learn about and practice using effective strategies.

Learning strategies can be a focal area for the first-year seminar course. Many first-year seminar courses have learning outcomes that specifically address the development and utilization of effective study approaches. Students taking the first-year seminar course can learn about which study approaches will best help them achieve their goals. Knowing the effectiveness of testing as a learning strategy, first-year seminar instructors can structure their class in a way that requires students to regularly engage in practice retrieval. This can be accomplished via a variety of techniques such as traditional quizzes, polling, or asking students to write brief summaries of content learned (Harrington & Zakrajsek, 2017).

In addition, first-year seminar instructors can encourage students to put the testing effect into practice outside of the classroom as well. For example, instructors can suggest or even provide incentives so that students take advantage of practice tests that are often available via publisher websites. This way, students can get feedback on their learning progress, make adjustments as needed, and benefit from engaging in practice retrieval. When practice tests are unavailable, students can be encouraged to create their own quizzes. Students may even opt to work with classmates in a study group where all members develop quiz questions, creating a large pool of questions the entire group can use to engage in practice retrieval.

Another great option is flashcards. Flashcards that contain a question or a vocabulary word on one side and the response or definition on the other side can provide students with an opportunity to put the testing effect into practice and establish strong foundational knowledge in that subject area. When using these techniques, students are engaging in practice retrieval of content previously learned and putting the testing effect into practice. This will help students remember content that will be needed later, especially when engaging in higher-level tasks.

Teaching to Learn

Teaching is another powerful learning strategy. When the goal is to teach someone else, students realize that this requires a significant amount of time and effort. As a result, deep-level learning is very likely when using teaching as a learning strategy. First-year seminars can be set up in a way that teaching is a central part of the learning experience. For example, the Jigsaw Classroom Activity could be used (Aronson, Blaney, Stephan, Sikes, & Snapp, 1978). This activity requires every member of a group to deeply explore and learn a specific subject area. After doing so, each group member needs to go back and teach other group members about the subject area they learned about.

Engaging in this teaching for learning process is extremely effective at building knowledge and skills. One concern often expressed about this approach is whether or not students are teaching accurate information. By using the teaching as a learning tool approach during class, the instructor is available to validate and confirm that the information being taught is accurate and useful. Thus, the instructor still has a very important role during the Jigsaw Classroom Activity.

First-year seminar instructors can also encourage students to use the teaching-to-learn strategy outside of the classroom. For example, students can be encouraged to work with classmates in a study group where members take turns teaching one another content or a student can be encouraged to teach a friend, family member, or significant other content learned in class or from the readings. First-year instructors can increase the likelihood that students will use this teaching-to-learn approach by giving students class time to discover the value of and develop skills related to teaching as a learning tool.

Organizing Strategies

Making connections and organizing concepts is another learning approach that is strongly supported by research. Putting information into your own words and finding connections between different concepts is a way to engage in deep learning. These activities require active learning on the part of the student, moving beyond passive approaches such as reviewing. Although students may know that these techniques are effective, many students are not regularly using organizing strategies.

In an interesting study by Dickinson and O'Connell (1990), it was found that high-performing and low-performing students were similar in terms of how much time they spent reading and reviewing course content, but that high-performers were more likely to use organizing strategies. In this study, organizing was defined as students putting information in their own words, using a hierarchical structure to make connections between concepts, and creating examples of concepts.

The in and out of class activities in a first-year seminar course can help students develop behaviors and study practices that emphasize organizing strategies. During class, first-year seminar instructors can ask students to create concept maps related to the course content or identify examples. After class, students can be encouraged to repackage their class and reading notes into a matrix or table and identify additional examples of the content just learned.

Spaced Practice

Although the type of study strategy really matters, how these strategies are utilized also matters. Students who use the spaced approach study numerous times over a long period of time, while students who use the massed approach study all of the content in a short amount of time. There is much research that shows that students who engage in spaced versus massed practice perform better (Schwartz et al., 2011). Researchers have found that "the simple act of spacing out study and practice in installments and allowing time to elapse between them makes both the learning and the memory stronger" (Brown et al., 2014, p. 63). It is therefore important for students to learn the importance of spaced practice. In the first-year seminar course, instructors can share the research on spaced practice with students and assist students with developing a study plan that will result in high-level learning.

Self-Regulation

Fostering self-regulation skills is also important, especially early on in the college experience. When students effectively engage in self-regulation, they will be better able to determine if they are on track to meet their goal. Not surprisingly, self-regulation is linked to goal achievement. Students who engage in self-regulation seek out information that will help them monitor progress toward their goal, and they will then make adjustments as needed.

Although some students are skilled at self-regulation and engage in this process regularly, many students do not frequently engage in self-regulation, at least in an intentional way, and would benefit from assistance in this area. McGuire (2015) emphasizes how engaging in meta-cognitive, self-regulatory behaviors results in long-lasting learning. The first-year seminar is a perfect place to teach and support the use of self-regulation skills.

Even though the curriculum of the first-year seminar can explicitly address learning strategies, it is important to note that the development of learning skills takes time. Just like we would not expect all writing skills to be taught in an English course, academic success skills cannot be taught only in the first-year seminar. Institutions truly committed to student success need to foster and develop these skills throughout the curriculum.

Faculty teaching all classes can help students use effective learning strategies by designing courses in a way that encourages the use of these skills and by encouraging students to reach out for assistance as needed. Although the first-year seminar cannot by itself ensure that students are successful, it plays an incredibly important role in helping students build and develop a strong foundational knowledge in success skills, ensuring all students know how to use the learning strategies that work best. Using Guided Pathways terminology, the first-year seminar course can be used to help students stay on the path (Bailey et al., 2015).

BUILDING GRIT AND RESILIENCE

Helping students develop and use effective learning and study strategies is critical but not enough if we want to ensure that students continue on their path. Academic challenges are only one of the potential roadblocks to success. Unfortunately, many students, especially community college students, often withdraw from courses or programs for non-academic reasons such as family issues, stress, or emergencies (Pivik, 2015). O'Keefe (2013) notes that some populations such as students with disabilities, students from low socioeconomic situations, and students with mental health issues are often more likely to drop out and not complete college. Although colleges and universities may not have much control over other life factors that may prevent students from achieving their goals, courses such as the first-year seminar can be used to build grit and resilience.

Students who are more gritty and resilient will be more likely to persevere and achieve goals even in the face of obstacles and challenges. In fact, Duckworth, Peterson, Matthews, and Kelly (2007) found that grit, the ability to commit and continue to work on a goal despite challenges, predicted academic success better than intelligence did. Thus, building grit and resilience are essential components of keeping students on the path and getting students to the graduation finish line.

How do you build resilience and help students become gritty? Based on an extensive review of the research, Harrington (2019) noted that "Individuals who stick with tasks, have a positive and productive mindset, and a strong support system are much more likely to be resilient and gritty" (p. 222). Many first-year seminar courses address these issues, but often in a minimal way. Intentionally focusing on these factors throughout the entire semester rather than in an isolated lesson can increase the likelihood that students will truly build grit and resilience.

Persevering with Tasks

Not surprisingly, students will be more likely to stick with and complete activities when they place a high value on the task and are committed to completing the task successfully. Perkins-Gough (2013) notes that grit involves a high level of commitment to completing a task that results in individuals sticking with tasks over a long period of time. This high level of commitment is particularly critical when students face challenges or obstacles. It is therefore essential to emphasize the importance of commitment right from the start when students are establishing goals. Assisting students with developing high-level goals that they care about and are committed to seeing through to completion is an essential first step in building grit and resilience and is very much connected to being successful.

First-year seminar instructors can teach students about goal setting using a framework such as the ABCS model that incorporates commitment into the goal-setting process. According to the ABCS goal-setting framework, goal setting involves aiming high, believing in your ability to complete the goal successfully, caring about and being committed to your goal, specifying the outcome, and self-reflecting to monitor progress and make adjustments as needed (Harrington, 2019). During the first-year seminar, instructors can help students set goals according to this framework and engage students in regularly monitoring their progress.

It is important for the progress monitoring to go beyond simply documenting behaviors or actions related to achieving the goal; it must also tap into the level of motivation, challenging students to assess their level of care and commitment. This keeps the conversation about commitment and persistence an ongoing one, with numerous opportunities for intervention to increase the level of commitment and motivation if needed. Students who regularly revisit their motivational and commitment levels keep their goal front and center, and this makes success more likely.

Fostering a Positive and Productive Mindset

Beliefs matter. Cognitive psychologists have been researching the powerful role that thought plays in success for years (Seligman Steen, Park, & Peterson, 2005). Success is more likely when you and others you care about believe you will be successful, when you are optimistic about the future, and when you productively interpret mistakes (Carver, 1998; Grant & Dweck 2003; Henry, Martinko, & Pierce, 1993; Nes, Evans, & Segerstrom, 2009).

Teacher Beliefs

First and foremost, instructors need to believe in their students. This was demonstrated in a classic psychological experiment conducted by Rosenthal and Jacobson (1968). In this classic study, elementary school students were given an IQ test, but their actual IQ was not shared with anyone. Teachers received class rosters with fake IQ scores that were randomly assigned to students. It is important to note that only the teachers knew the fake IQ scores.

At the end of the experiment, the students who were initially labeled "smart" via a high fake IQ score had higher IQ scores than the students who were initially labeled "not smart" via a low fake IQ score despite there being no difference in their IQ at the start of the study. The only difference between the two groups of students was whether their teacher believed in them because of the randomly assigned IQ scores. This experiment, which would be considered unethical by today's standards, demonstrated how teacher expectations impacted student performance. It is therefore critical that we begin by believing in students.

Self-Efficacy

Students also need to believe in themselves. Students who believe in their ability to be successful are more likely to set higher goals, put forth more effort, and continue to persevere on a task (Bandura, 1997). Believing in your ability to be successful is a concept called self-efficacy. High self-efficacy is particularly important when encountering difficulties or obstacles. This was illustrated in a study by Komarraju and Nadler (2013) who found that students with high self-efficacy were more likely to persevere with tasks even when faced with failure or difficulties.

It can be argued that building self-efficacy is one of the most important learning objectives of the first-year seminar course. Recognizing the importance of self-efficacy, first-year seminar course coordinators from community colleges in New Jersey decided to begin all learning outcomes for the course with a stem that focused on building self-efficacy. More specifically, the stem preceding all learning outcomes is as follows: "Students will develop a higher sense of self-efficacy by _____ " (Center for Student Success at the New Jersey Council of County Colleges, n.d.).

The best way to build self-efficacy is through successful experiences. This was illustrated in a study by Kudo and Mori (2015) where students who directly experienced success with an anagram task had higher levels of self-efficacy as compared to those who did not experience success with this task. First-year seminar instructors can therefore play an important role in building student self-efficacy by designing challenging but doable assignments and providing the right level of support to assist students with being successful. It is important to note that success on an assignment that is low-level or not challenging does not build self-efficacy, so instructors need not lower standards or assign "easy" tasks. Rather, the key is high-level performance on tasks that are perceived to be challenging.

To assist students with being successful on high-level tasks, the first-year seminar instructor can support the student by teaching skills and strategies needed for success and by providing meaningful feedback regularly. For example, let's assume that the students in the class need to do a presentation. The first-year seminar instructor can teach information literacy skills to assist the student with finding the best sources of information, can provide students with the opportunity to learn and practice effective reading strategies to increase understanding of the content, can teach students about evidence-based multi-media principles, and can provide feedback on content and slides prior to the presentation. The skills learned in the first-year seminar course will serve the student well in other courses too, building self-efficacy in many academic areas.

Optimism

In addition to believing in one's ability to be successful, having a positive mindset about the future in general also fosters resilience and grit (Duckworth, 2016). Believing that the future will be positive is often referred to as optimism. Many refer to optimistic individuals as "glass-half-full" type people, who see the world from a positive lens. In this glass-half-full analogy, individuals could describe a glass that contains half water and half air as either half full or half empty. Both would be accurate statements, but looking at the situation from a positive angle, noting what is there versus what is not there has been linked to positive outcomes. Optimism can be learned (Foregard & Seligman, 2012) and has been found to be a strong predictor of resilience and success, especially among first-year college students (Dawson & Pooley, 2013).

Growth Mindset

Relatedly, there has also been an extensive amount of research on the powerful role that growth mindset plays in success (Dweck, Waltron, & Cohen, 2014). Individuals with a growth mindset believe that intelligence is not fixed and that one can become more intelligent through practice and effort. When students believe in the growth mindset, they will be more likely to engage in actions that will result in increased learning. Students who, on the other hand, believe that intelligence is fixed will be more likely to give up after a failure experience. It is therefore important for first-year seminar instructors to teach students about growth mindset and to engage in behaviors that will foster this productive mindset. This can have positive, long-lasting benefits for students.

Attributions

Interpreting failures productively is a key component of developing a positive and industrious mindset. It is critical that students attribute their successes and failures to internal factors that they believe they can control or influence. For example, when students attribute success and failure to effort, they will be more likely to put forth higher levels of effort in the future in order to successfully complete a task (Mueller & Dweck, 1998). On the other hand, if students view the failure experience as one that they do not have any control over, they will be more likely to give up or not put forth much effort. Believing you influenced the outcome refers to an internal locus of control and researchers have consistently found that an internal locus of control is linked to positive outcomes such as high-level performance on academic tasks (Stupniskey et al., 2007).

The good news is that individuals can be taught to be more positive and productive in their thinking. This was illustrated in a study conducted by Feldman and Dreher (2012) where students who participated in a training session on hope did in fact have higher levels of hope at the conclusion of the session. In another study, Mueller and Dweck (1998) found that telling students they were successful because they worked hard positively impacted their performance on a related task in the future.

In other words, directing student attention to how their actions impact performance leads to better outcomes. It is important to note, however, that simply telling students to work harder may not lead to improved performance and in some cases, can frustrate students who are putting forth a significant amount of effort. Instead of suggesting that students work harder, help students identify specific learning strategies that they can use to improve their performance.

The first-year seminar is an excellent place to foster a positive and productive mindset. First-year instructors can create a climate that is positive in nature and that places high importance on having a positive mindset. Specifically, instructors can share the research on growth mindset and optimism, encourage students to regularly write or share positive experiences, identify the actions they took to create successful outcomes, provide feedback that focuses on their actions, and inspire students to think and speak positively about their goals. It is important to note that addressing the powerful role of mindset throughout the semester, especially when students receive feedback on assignments, rather than treating mindset as a topic to be covered during a class period is much more likely to contribute to high levels of resilience and grit.

Developing and Strengthening Relationships

Support systems are also critical in building resilience and grit. A significant body of research has demonstrated the important role that a sense of belonging or connection has to academic performance and persistence (Tinto, 1993). Student-student and student-faculty relationships significantly impact a student's sense of belonging.

Hoffman, Richmond, Morrow, and Salomone (2002), for instance, discovered that students who developed supportive peer relationships and believed that faculty knew who they were and cared about them were more likely to persist in college. Research has demonstrated that sense of belonging predicts persistence even after accounting for several other variables that typically play a role in persistence (Hausman, Schofield, & Woods, 2007). In this research study, institutional interventions, such as college administrators frequently communicating to students and providing students with small gifts that display the college logo, positively impacted students' sense of belonging. It is therefore very possible for an institution to increase a student's sense of belonging.

Friedman (2017) notes that one of the primary reasons that the first-year seminar has been able to positively impact persistence rates and success is because it fosters a strong sense of belonging among peers and a faculty member. The first-year seminar curriculum has a personal focus that allows students to more easily connect with one another. Having at least one strong relationship with a peer, professor, or staff person can make a huge difference in terms of persistence.

According to results from a national survey, "most continuing students indicate that, at some point, they considered dropping out, and their reasons for staying in school are revealing: They almost always include the name of a particular person—an instructor, a staff member, another student—who gave the encouragement, guidance, or support they needed to keep going" (Center for Community College Student Engagement, 2009). It is therefore critical that students make connections with others. While it can be easier for students who live in residence halls to make connections to their peers, it can be more challenging for commuter students to do so. For commuter students, it is even more important to focus on fostering connections in the classroom.

Building Supportive Relationships Inside the Classroom

The classroom is the common experience for all students and a great place for students to connect with peers and their professor. For commuter students, the classroom is the primary opportunity to develop relationships with other students. Unfortunately, many students may not interact much, if at all, with their classmates and professor during class.

Building a sense of community in all classes is important, but it is especially important and sometimes easier to do in a first-year seminar course given the personal focus of this course. Friedman (2017) noted that long-lasting connections with others are easier to make in a first-year seminar course due to the personal focus of the course. Because the content focus is student success, students taking the first-year seminar can share and discuss personal, academic, and career goals, and doing so can help students get to know one another in personally meaningful ways.

First-year instructors can facilitate strong peer-to-peer relationships through classroom activities that require students to interact with one another. At the beginning of the semester, instructors can ask students to engage in icebreaker activities to help them get to know one another. Icebreaker activities, such as the Jigsaw Classroom Syllabus activity described by Harrington and Thomas (2018), can help students get to know one another while also getting familiar with the course goals and structure.

Although icebreakers are very useful for developing a comfortable learning environment where students get to know one another, having students work on more in-depth learning projects in small groups can be more important when it comes to building strong peer connections. Millis (2002), however, points out that that all group work is not equally productive and useful. Simply putting students in groups will not always lead to positive peer-to-peer connections, and it is of course possible for students to have negative experiences in groups that result in conflict rather than support.

First-year seminar instructors can facilitate positive student-to-student interactions by teaching students how to function productively in a group. More specifically, first-year seminar instructors can share the 5R approach to group work: establish rapport, determine rules, determine roles, get ready to work and support one another, and remember to evaluate (Harrington, 2019). When students learn these essential group skills, they will be more productive and more likely to develop good relationships with their peers.

First-year instructors can also help students develop these essential skills by having students engage in group work during class. This way, first-year instructors can see firsthand how students are functioning and can intervene as needed to support more productive group behaviors. Creating a learning environment where students know and support one another can contribute to successful outcomes.

In addition to teaching students how to function productively in a group, it is also important for first-year instructors to carefully craft group learning tasks. First-year instructors using backward design principles described by Wiggins and McTighe (2005) determine which teaching methods will best help students achieve the course learning outcomes. When group work is determined to be the best approach, instructors can then carefully design the learning task, providing students with a clear overview and purpose for the task. In addition, the group work can be designed so that all members of the group must work collaboratively, with each member individually accountable (Millis, 2002). This approach to group work increases the likelihood that students will have a positive experience and establish meaningful connections with peers.

Building Supportive Relationships Outside the Classroom

Although it is important to help students build connections in the classroom, getting students involved outside of the classroom is also important. For example, when students participate in campus activities and organizations, they are more likely to develop strong relationships with peers and feel like they belong and are a part of the college or university. Research conducted by Strap and Farr (2010) found that out-of-class experiences and activities play a critical role in success outcomes.

Despite the advantages of being involved and the numerous opportunities for students to participate in clubs and organizations on college campuses, not all students opt to get involved. Two often-cited reasons that students give for not getting involved are not having enough time and not seeing the value of participating. First-generation students are often less likely than their peers to get involved because of these reasons. Pascarella, Pierson, Wolniak, and Terenzini (2004) note that "involvement during college may be a particularly useful way for first-generation students to acquire the additional cultural capital that helps them succeed academically and benefit cognitively" (p. 278).

How can we increase the number of students who take advantage of outside-of-class activities that can foster resilience and build grit? One way is to increase awareness of options and share the value of participating with students. Knowing the importance of engaging with others outside of the classroom, first-year instructors have long shared information about ways of getting involved and the value and benefits associated with participating in clubs and organizations. Many first-year instructors even invite someone from the student activities office to speak to the class and share information about how to get involved on campus, or the instructor may bring their class to the annual student activities fair.

Another approach used by many first-year seminar instructors is to require (or give extra credit to) students who explore their options and attend at least a few events or club meetings on campus. Kay McClenney strongly advises colleges and universities to require students to participate in outside-of-class activities that have a demonstrated link to success (Fain, 2012). Although some students won't need the extrinsic motivator of a grade or extra credit, for other students, this may be exactly what is needed to make getting involved a priority.

The truth is that we communicate priorities through our grading systems. First-year seminar instructors can create assignments related to getting involved outside the classroom to foster relationships and help students become more resilient and gritty. Relationships that are formed as a result of these initial actions can often be long-lasting, establishing a support system that can serve students well throughout their college experience and beyond.

Having strong support is most critical when they encounter challenges and stressful situations. Students who have a solid support system are more likely to be resilient. In many cases, having even just one friend or family member to lean on in difficult times can be enough (Swenson, Nordstrom, & Hiester, 2008; Wintre & Yaffe, 2000). However, there may be some situations where current levels of support are not enough. In these cases, it can be helpful to expand current support systems to also include professionals.

Research has shown that students who reach out for assistance when needed are more successful than students who do not access support (Raskind, Goldberg, Higgins, & Herman, 1999). For example, when a student is experiencing a stressful personal situation, a professional mental health provider such as a psychologist or counselor can provide much needed support and guidance. Similarly, a student struggling with an academic task can benefit by accessing help from a professor, tutor, or librarian. Despite the usefulness of accessing help, the unfortunate truth is that many students do not seek out assistance from professionals on campus.

There are many reasons for students not accessing help. Some reasons include not recognizing the need for help, a lack of knowledge about resources, feeling uncomfortable with asking a stranger for help, and cultural values that do not encourage the seeking of outside help. Research conducted by Garriott, Raque-Bogdan, Yalango, Ziemer, and Utley (2017) emphasized how stigma associated with help-seeking is often what prevents students from reaching out for help, especially among first-generation college students.

In many of these cases, the first-year instructor can increase the likelihood that students will access help. For starters, students can learn about the various supports available on campus, and how to access these supports in the first-year seminar course. It can be particularly useful to have peers, upper-level college students, talk with first-year students about the value of accessing resources.

In addition to highlighting the importance of seeking help when needed, this approach can also reduce stigma related to help-seeking. Research shows that students who are more knowledgeable about resources will be more likely to access help when needed (Pace, Silk, Nazione, Fournier, & Collins-Eaglin, 2018). In addition, first-year seminar instructors can recognize when students need additional support and personally connect students to professionals on campus who can be of assistance.

Faculty are often the ones who are first to know if something may be interfering with a student's success. Because strong professor-student relationships are often formed in the first-year seminar, first-year seminar instructors are often the first to notice when a student is in need of additional support. In some cases, the student may approach the first-year seminar instructor to ask for help because a strong faculty-student relationship has been established. In other cases, the first-year seminar instructor may need to watch for behaviors that could indicate high levels of stress such as missed assignments, missing class or being late, or acting differently. In either case, first-year seminar instructors can listen and then connect the student to a helpful campus resource.

Because of the focus on student success in this course, first-year seminar instructors typically have a good understanding of campus resources. Instructors not only know about resources, they often personally know the professionals working in the various campus departments. These personal connections with professionals across the campus are significantly important. Students are more likely to use other resources when someone they trust makes a personal recommendation to a person rather than a general referral to an office. First-year seminar instructors can help students become familiar with campus resources through assignments, guest lectures, and most importantly through conversations about specific concerns and needs.

Knowing campus resources and connecting students to these resources is important, but it is not enough. The first-year seminar can also be used as a vehicle to build resilience and grit. More specifically, it can be very helpful for students to understand the importance of a positive mindset, strong support system, and a persistent attitude. Although we can't always control the events that happen in the lives of our students, we can help them control how they respond or react to the events.

Research has demonstrated that brief interventions aimed at building resilience and grit really do work. For example, Perry, Stupnisky, Hall, Chipperfield, & Weiner (2010) found that students who participated in a one-hour session on the importance of focusing on internal, changeable factors when interpreting success and failure had grade point averages that were almost one letter grade higher than their peers who did not participate in this training. These results are extremely promising and show the value of even brief interventions that can be easily incorporated into first-year seminar courses.

During this class, first-year seminar instructors can help students interpret feedback productively and assist students with determining the most appropriate next step or action. In addition to assisting students with developing a positive, productive mindset, the first-year seminar course is also a great place to develop and foster relationships, which is also an essential factor of being resilient and gritty.

In a research study conducted by Rahat and Ilhan (2016), for instance, it was found that social support was a key resilient factor for first-year college students. Given the important role of relationships in grit and resilience, having an entire first-year seminar course, rather than a few isolated student success workshops, is recommended. Throughout the semester, students taking a first-year seminar course develop strong relationships with peers and their professor. Although these relationships are of course possible in all courses, the personal nature of this course makes the development of relationships more likely and long-lasting.

In summary, colleges and universities can use first-year seminars as an opportunity to help students develop the necessary learning strategies needed for success, develop a positive, productive mindset, and connect with peers, their professor, and campus resources as needed. Students who develop a strong set of academic skills and behaviors that are grounded in theory and research are more likely to meet with success (Harrington, 2019). In addition, other key success factors such as resilience and grit can be fostered and developed in the first-year seminar.

REFERENCES

Anderson, L., & Krathwohl, D. A. (2001). *Taxonomy for learning, teaching and assessing: A revision of Bloom's Taxonomy of Educational Objectives*. New York: Longman.

Aronson, E., Blaney, N., Stephan, C., Sikes, J., & Snapp, M. (1978) *The jigsaw classroom*. Beverly Hills, CA: Sage.

Baddeley, A. D. (2002). Is working memory still working? *European Psychologist, 7*(2), 85–97. doi:10.1027//1016-9040.7.2.85

Bailey, T. R., Smith Jaggars, S., & Jenkins, D. (2015). *Redesigning America's community colleges: A clearer path to student success*. Cambridge, MA: Harvard University Press.

Bandura, A. (1977). *Social learning theory*. Englewood Cliffs, NJ: Prentice Hall.

Bandura, A. (1997). *Self-efficacy: The exercise of control*. New York: Freeman.

Bers, T., Chun, M., Daly, W. T., Harrington, C., Toblowsky, B. F., & Associates (2015). *Foundations for critical thinking*. Columbia, SC: University of South Carolina, National Resource Center for The First-Year Experience and Students in Transition.

Bloom, B. S. (Ed.). (1956). *Taxonomy of educational objectives: The classification of educational goals; Handbook I: Cognitive domain*. White Plains, NY: Longmans, Green.

Brown, P. C., Roediger III, H. L., & McDaniel (2014). *Make it stick: The science of successful learning.* Cambridge, MA: The Belknap Press of Harvard University Press.

Brownson, C., Becker, M. S., Shadick, R., Jaggars, S. S., & Nitkin-Kaner, Y. (2014). Suicidal behavior and help seeking among diverse college students. *Journal of College Counseling, 17*(2), 116–130. doi:10.1002/j.2161-1882.2014.00052.x

Carver, C. S. (1998). Resilience and thriving: Issues, models, and linkages. *Journal of Social Issues, 54*(2), 245–266.Retrieved from Academic Search Premiere database.

Center for Community College Student Engagement. (2009). *Making connections: Dimensions of student engagement (2009 CCSSE Findings).* Austin, TX: The University of Texas at Austin, Community College Leadership Program.

Center for Student Success at the New Jersey Council of County Colleges. (n.d.). *A Guided Pathways framework.* Retrieved from http://www.njstudentsuccess.com

Dawson, M., & Pooley, J. A. (2013). Resilience: The role of optimism, perceived parental autonomy support and perceived social support in first-year university students. *Journal of Education and Training Studies, 1*(2), 38–49.

DeBerard, M. S., Spielmans, G. I., & Julka, D. L. (2004). Predictors of academic achievement and retention among college freshmen: A longitudinal study. *College Student Journal, 38*(1), 66–80.

Dickinson, D. J., & O'Connell, D. Q. (1990). Effect of quality and quantity of study on student grades. *Journal of Educational Research, 83*(4), 227.

Duckworth, A. (2016). *Grit: The power of passion and perseverance.* New York: Scribner.

Duckworth, A. L., Peterson, C., Matthews, M. D., & Kelly, D. R. (2007). Grit: Perseverance and passion for long-term goals. *Journal of Personality and Social Psychology, 92*(6), 1087–1101.

Dunlosky, J., Rawson, K. A., Marsh, E. J., Nathan, M. J., & Willingham, D. T. (2013). Improving students' learning with effective learning techniques: Promising directions from cognitive and educational psychology. *Psychological Science in The Public Interest, 14*(1), 4–58. doi:10.1177/1529100612453266

Dweck, C., Walton, G., & Cohen, G. (2014). *Academic tenacity: Mindsets and skills that promote long-term learning.* Bill & Melinda Gates Foundation.

Einstein, G. O., Mullet, H. G., & Harrison, T. L. (2012). The testing effect: Illustrating a fundamental concept and changing study strategies. *Teaching of Psychology, 39*(3), 190–193.

Fain, P. (2012, February 2) Make it mandatory? Inside Higher Education. Retrieved from https://www.insidehighered.com/news/2012/02/02/academic-support-offerings-go-unused-community-colleges

Feldman, D. B., & Dreher, D. E. (2012). Can hope be changed in 90 minutes? Testing the efficacy of a single-session goal-pursuit intervention for college students. *Journal of Happiness Studies, 13*(4), 745–759. doi: 0.1007/s10902-011-9292-4

Foregard, M. C., & Seligman, M. P. (2012). Seeing the glass half full: A review of the causes and consequences of optimism. *Pratiques Psychologiques, 18*(2), 107–120. doi: 10.1016/j-prps.2012.02.002

Friedman, D. (2017, December). *First-year experience: Engaging students through active learning.* Presented at the New Jersey Center for Student Success, Edison, NJ.

Garriott, P. O., Raque-Bogdan, T. L., Yalango, K., Ziemer, K. S., & Utley, J. (2017). Intentions to seek counseling in first-generation and continuing-generation college students. *Journal of Counseling Psychology, 64*(4), 432–442. doi:10.1037/cou0000210

Goswami, U. (2008). Principles of learning, implications for teaching: A cognitive neuroscience perspective. *Journal of Philosophy of Education,* 42(3-4), 381–399.

Grant, H., & Dweck, C. S. (2003). Clarifying achievement goals and their impact. *Journal of Personality and Social Psychology, 85*(3), 541–553. doi:10.1037/0022-3514.85.3.541

Grillo, M. C., & Leist, C. W. (2013). Academic support as a predictor of retention to graduation: New insights on the role of tutoring, learning assistance, and supplemental instruction. *Journal of College Student Retention: Research, Theory and Practice, 15*(3), 387–408. doi:10.2190/CS.15.3.e

Harrington, C. (2019). *Student success in college: Doing what works!* (3rd ed.). Boston, MA: Cengage.

Harrington, C., & Thomas, M. (2018). *Designing a motivational syllabus: Creating a learning path for student engagement.* Sterling, VA: Stylus.

Harrington, C., & Zakrajsek, T. (2017). *Dynamic lecturing: Research-based strategies to enhance lecture effectiveness.* Sterling, VA: Stylus.

Hausmann, L. M., Schofield, J. W., & Woods, R. L. (2007). Sense of belonging as a predictor of intentions to persist among African American and White first-year college students. *Research in Higher Education, 48*(7), 803–839.

Henry, J., Martinko, M., & Pierce, M. (1993). Attributional style as a predictor of success in a first computer course. *Computers in Human Behavior, 9*(4), 341–352. doi:10.1016/0747-5632(93)90027-P

Hoffman, M., Richmond, J., Morrow, J., & Salomone, K. (2002). Investigating "sense of belonging" in first-year college students. *Journal of College Student Retention: Research, Theory and Practice, 4*(3), 227–256. doi:10.2190/DRYC-CXQ9-JQ8V-HT4V

Karp, M. M., & Stacey, G. W. (2013). What we know about nonacademic student supports. *Community College Research Center, Teachers College, Columbia University.* Retrieved from https://ccrc.tc.columbia.edu/publications/what-we-know-student-supports.html

King, A. (1995). Designing the instructional process to enhance critical thinking across the curriculum—Inquiring minds really do want to know: Using questioning to teach critical thinking. *Teaching of Psychology, 22*(1), 13–17.

Komarraju, M., & Nadler, D. (2013). Self-efficacy and academic achievement: Why do implicit beliefs, goals, and effort regulation matter? *Learning and Individual Differences, 25,* 67–72.

Krumrei-Mancuso, E. J., Newton, F. B., Kim, E., & Wilcox, D. (2013). Psychosocial factors predicting first-year college student success. *Journal of College Student Development, 54*(3), 247–266. Retrieved from ERIC database.

Kudo, H., & Mori, K. (2015). A preliminary study of increasing self-efficacy in junior high school students: Induced success and a vicarious experience. *Psychological Reports, 117*(2), 631–642. doi:10.2466/11.07.PR0.117c22z4

Lynch, D. J. (2006). Motivational strategies, learning strategies, and resource management as predictors of course grades. *College Student Journal, 40*(2), 423–428. Retrieved from Academic Search Premiere database.

Mabel, Z., & Britton, T. A. (2018). Leaving late: Understanding the extent and predictors of college late departure. *Social Science Research,* 69, 34–51. doi:10.1016/j.ssresearch.2017.10.001

McGuire, S. Y. (2015). *Teaching students how to learn: Strategies you can incorporate into any course to improve student metacognition, study skills, and motivation.* Sterling, VA: Stylus.

Millis, B. J. (2002). Enhancing learning-and more! Through cooperative learning. IDEA Paper #38. Retrieved from http://www.theideacenter.org/sites/default/files/IDEA_Paper_38.pdf

Mueller, C. M., & Dweck, C. S. (1998). Praise for intelligence can undermine children's motivation and performance. *Journal of Personality and Social Psychology, 75*(1), 33–52. Retrieved from PsycInfo database.

National Academic Advising Association (NACADA, 2011). 2011 NACADA national survey of academic advising. Retrieved from http://www.nacada.ksu.edu/Resources/Clearinghouse/View-Articles/2011-NACADA-National-Survey.aspx

Nes, L., Evans, D. R., & Segerstrom, S. C. (2009). Optimism and college retention: Mediation by motivation, performance, and adjustment. *Journal of Applied Social Psychology, 39*(8), 1887–1912. doi:10.1111/j.1559-1816.2009.00508.x

O'Keefe, P. (2013). A sense of belonging: Improving student retention. *College Student Journal, 47*(4), 605–613.

Ozuru, Y., Dempsey, K., & McNamara, D. S. (2009). Prior knowledge, reading skill, and text cohesion in the comprehension of science texts. *Learning and Instruction, 19*(3), 228–242. doi:10.1016/j.learninstruc.2008.04.003

Pace, K., Silk, K., Nazione, S., Fournier, L., & Collins-Eaglin, J. (2018). Promoting mental health help seeking behavior among first-year college students. *Health Communication, 33*(2), 102–110. doi:10.1080/10410236.2016.1250065

Pascarella, E. T., Pierson, C. T., Wolniak, G. C., & Terenzini, P. T. (2004). First-generation college students: Additional evidence on college experiences and outcomes. *Journal of Higher Education, 75*(3), 249–284.

Pashler, H., McDaniel, M., Rohrer, D., & Bjork, R. (2008). Learning styles: Concepts and evidence. *Psychological Science in the Public Interest, 9*(3), 105–119. doi:10.1111/j.1539.6053.2009.01038.

Perkins-Gough, D. (2013). The significance of grit: A conversation with Angela Lee Duckworth. *Educational Leadership, 71*(1), 14–20.

Perry, R. P., Stupnisky, R. H., Hall, N. C., Chipperfield, J. G., & Weiner, B. (2010). Bad starts and better finishes: Attributional retraining and initial performance in competitive achievement settings. *Journal of Social and Clinical Psychology, 29*(6), 668–700. Retrieved from Academic Search Premier database.

Pivik, B. (2015, November 11). Top 11 reasons why college students drop out: Don't let it happen to you. Retrieved from https://blog.petersons.com/2015/11/11/top-11-reasons-why-college-students-dropout-dont-let-it-happen-to-you/

Rahat, E., & Ilhan, T. (2016). Coping styles, social support, relational self-construal, and resilience in predicting students' adjustment to university life. *Educational Sciences: Theory and Practice, 16*(1), 187–208.

Raskind, M. H., Goldberg, R. J., Higgins, E. L., & Herman, K. L. (1999). Patterns of change and predictors of success in individuals with learning disabilities: Results from a twenty-year longitudinal study. *Learning Disabilities Research and Practice, 14*, 35–49. doi:10.1207/sldrp1401_4

Roediger, H., & Karpicke, J. D. (2006). Test-enhanced learning: Taking memory tests improves long-term retention. *Psychological Science, 17*(3), 249–255. doi:10.1111/j.1467-9280.2006.01693.x

Rosenthal, R., & Jacobson, L. (1968). *Pygmalion in the classroom: Teacher expectation and pupils' intellectual development.* Bethel, CT: Crown House Publishing.

Ryan, M. (2013). Improving retention and academic achievement for first-time students at a two-year college. *Community College Journal of Research & Practice, 37*(2), 130–134. doi:10.1080/10668926.2012.715266

Ryan, M. P. & Glenn, P. A. (2004). What do first-year students need most: Learning strategies instruction or academic socialization? *Journal of College Reading and Learning, 34*(2), 4–28.

Schwartz, B. L., Son, L. K., Kornell, N., & Finn, B. (2011). Four principles of memory improvement: A guide to improving learning efficiency. *The International Journal of Creativity and Problem Solving, 21*(1), 7–15.

Schwitzer, A. M. (2005). Self-development, social support, and student help-seeking: Research summary and implications for college psychotherapists. *Journal of College Student Psychotherapy, 20*(2), 29–52. doi:10.1300/J035v20n02_04

Seligman, M., Steen, T., Park, N., & Peterson, C. (2005). Positive psychology progress: Empirical validation of interventions. *American Psychologist, 60*(5), 410–421. doi:10.1037/0003-066X.60.5.410

Stanovich, K. E. (2008). Matthew effects in reading: Some consequences of individual differences in the acquisition of literacy. *Journal of Education, 189*(1/2), 23–55.

Strap, C. M., & Farr, R. J. (2010). To get involved or not: The relation among extracurricular involvement, satisfaction, and academic achievement. *Teaching of Psychology, 37*(1), 50–54. doi:10.1080/00986280903425870

Stupnisky, R., Renaud, R., Perry, R., Ruthig, J., Haynes, T., & Clifton, R. (2007). Comparing self-esteem and perceived control as predictors of first-year college students' academic achievement. *Social Psychology of Education, 10*(3), 303–330. doi:10.1007/s11218-007-9020-4

Swenson, L., Nordstrom, A., & Hiester, M. (2008). The role of peer relationships in adjustment to college. *Journal of College Student Development, 49*(6), 551–567. doi:10.1353/csd.0.0038

Tinto, V. (1993). Leaving college: Rethinking the causes and cures of student attrition (2nd ed.). University of Chicago Press, Chicago.

U.S. Department of Education, National Center for Education Statistics. (2017). The condition of education 2017 (NCES 2017-144), Undergraduate Retention and Graduation Rates.

Vertsberger, D., & Gati, I. (2015). The effectiveness of sources of support in career decision making: A two-year follow up. *Journal of Vocational Behavior, 89*, 151–161. doi: 10.1016/j.jvb.2015.06.004

Wiggins, G., & McTighe, J. (2005). Understanding by design (expanded 2nd ed.) Upper Saddle River, NJ: Pearson.

Willingham, D. T. (2009). *Why don't students like school? A cognitive scientist answers questions about how the mind works and what it means for the classroom.* San Francisco: Jossey Bass.

Wintre, M., & Yaffe, M. (2000). First-year students' adjustment to university life as a function of relationships with parents. *Journal of Adolescent Research, 15*(1), 9–37. doi:10.1177/0743558400151002

Woosley, S. A., & Miller, A. L. (2009). Integration and institutional commitment as predictors of college student transition: Are third-week indicators significant? *College Student Journal, 43*(4), 1260–1271.

Yang, Y.-T. C., Newby, T. J., & Bill, R. L. (2005). Using Socratic questioning to promote critical thinking skills through asynchronous discussion forums in distance learning environments. *American Journal of Distance Education, 19*(3), 163–181. doi:10.1207/s15389286ajde1903_4

Young, D. G., & Hopp, J. M. (2014). *2012–2013 National Survey of First-Year Seminars: Exploring high impact practices in the first college year* (Research Report No. 4). Columbia, SC: University of South Carolina, National Resource Center for The First-Year Experience & Students in Transition.

Part II

Practical Guide to Reimagining the First-Year Seminar Course within the Guided Pathways Framework

Chapter Five

Reimagining and Strengthening the First-Year Seminar Course

The Course Redesign Process

First-year seminars can vary significantly from college to college and even sometimes within the same institution. According to results from a national survey on the first-year seminar, the type of course and the type of institution can influence the focus of this course (Young & Hopp, 2014).

Not surprisingly, first-year seminars that were developed as an extended orientation experience were more likely to have a learning outcome focused on making a connection with the institution; while first-year seminars that were developed as discipline-specific courses were more likely to have a learning outcome focused on introducing students to an academic discipline. Young and Hopp (2014) also found differences between two-year and four-year institutions. For example, two-year colleges were more likely to emphasize study skills as a learning outcome (44.7%) as compared to four-year colleges and universities (11.9%).

Although learning goals can and do vary across institutions, there are some themes that emerge across most first-year seminar courses. "Efforts in the seminar appear to be aimed at assisting students to develop a connection with the institution, providing orientation to campus resources and services, and developing academic skills" (Young & Hopp, 2014, p. 29). These themes are commonly found in syllabi, textbooks, and other course materials.

Unfortunately, career exploration was not often cited as a focal area for learning outcomes in the first-year seminar course. Only 12.8% of two-year colleges and 4.2% of four-year colleges and universities indicated that career exploration and preparation was a focus of course learning outcomes (Young

& Hopp, 2014). Given the high number of students who are entering college undecided about a career path and the high number of students who change their major and career path, this is of concern. Bailey, Smith Jaggars, and Jenkins (2015) discuss how the first-year seminar can be used to help students choose and stay on a path. To actualize this vision, colleges and universities may need to revisit the purpose and goals of the first-year seminar course and engage in a course redesign process.

AN INTRODUCTION TO BACKWARD DESIGN

There is a significant body of research that supports the backward design approach to course design (Armbruster, Patel, Johnson, & Weiss, 2009; Reynolds & Kearns, 2017; Rienties & Toetenel, 2016; Wang, Su, Cheung, Wong, & Kwong, 2013). For example, effective course design has been linked to positive outcomes such as higher-level work produced by students, increased student confidence, and most importantly increased learning (Levine et al., 2008; Winkelmes et al., 2016). Although all students benefit, using an effective course design process such as backward design is particularly useful and helpful to first-generation students (Winkelmes et al., 2016). The backward design approach explicitly communicates the link between goals and assignments and students and this is particularly helpful to first-generation students. Effective course design can therefore be viewed as an effective way to address equity issues in higher education.

The backward course design process can best be summarized by designing a course with the end in mind (Wiggins & McTighe, 2005). In other words, faculty planning courses first think about the goals of the course. What will students be able to know, think, or do as a result of taking the course? These goals are then stated in action-oriented, measurable statements that are often referred to as learning outcomes. Learning outcomes drive the course design process so it is essential that faculty focus on determining the course outcomes prior to considering assessment activities and teaching methods.

To clearly articulate the learning goals, faculty often turn to Bloom's 1956 taxonomy for guidance. According to Bloom's taxonomy, which was revised by Anderson and Krathwohl (2001), there are six levels of knowing: remembering, understanding, applying, analyzing, evaluating, and creating. By focusing attention on the various levels of knowing, it can be easier for faculty to communicate the learning expectations. For example, some learning outcomes may focus on building basic foundational knowledge and therefore would be aligned to the remembering and understanding levels; while other learning outcomes may target higher-level cognitive skills such as applying, evaluating, or analyzing.

Typically, three to five major learning outcomes are identified for each course. More specific learning objectives can then be identified for each class or module within each course. Learning objectives are narrower in scope but connected to overall learning outcomes for the course. For example, a learning outcome might be "Creating academic, career and financial plans" (Center for Student Success at New Jersey Council of County Colleges, n.d.) and a few associated learning objectives could be to "Identify strengths, values and interests as they relate to careers," "Locate and evaluate career information," and "Determine academic requirements needed to graduate with a degree in desired field."

Both learning outcomes and learning objectives need to be measurable. Bloom's (1956) taxonomy can be a useful tool for objectives as well as outcomes. There are many online resources available that provide faculty with guidance and suggestions on how to use Bloom's taxonomy to create well-written learning objectives. In many cases, learning outcomes and possibly even learning objectives may be determined at a state-wide or department-wide level. In other words, instructors do not always need to develop the learning outcomes. In this situation, instructors can start with the next step of the process: determining what evidence will demonstrate that the students achieved the learning outcomes.

Harrington and Thomas (2018) note that course-level learning outcomes need to connect to program learning outcomes. In other words, courses are a part of an overall curriculum and every course in the curriculum needs to support the overall goals of the program or major. It is therefore important for faculty to consider each course within the context of the overall program. It can even be helpful to map out or explicitly show how course learning outcomes are connected to program learning outcomes.

After learning outcomes and objectives are identified, faculty can consider what type of evidence is needed to know whether or not students have successfully achieved the course learning outcomes. Thus, the second step in the backward design process is determining appropriate types of evidence. In other words, the focus shifts to figuring out which assignments can be best used as evidence. For example, a paper, project, or exam can be used to determine if students have achieved the learning outcomes.

It is important to be sure that assignments for every learning outcome are identified; otherwise, it will not be possible to determine if students were successful at achieving all the learning outcomes. It is not necessary, however, to have a different assignment for each learning outcome. Some assignments can be used to assess more than one learning outcome. In fact, this is advisable whenever possible.

The final step in the backward design process is identifying the teaching methods that will best assist students with performing well on the identified assignments and thus achieving the course learning outcomes. Different teaching approaches can work well for different types of learning outcomes. For example, the lecture can be very effective at building a strong base of foundational knowledge in a discipline while group work might be best for learning outcomes that emphasize the development of interpersonal or leadership skills. During this final phase of the process, faculty can develop lesson plans that articulate the specific teaching techniques that will be used during each class or module.

ESTABLISHING A COURSE DESIGN TEAM

Before engaging in course design, it is important to consider who should be involved in this process. Course design processes can vary from institution to institution. At many colleges and universities, a team of faculty from a discipline work together to determine the core elements of course design such as the learning outcomes. This could even happen at the state level for colleges and universities who are part of a state system.

In some cases, this collaborative process results in a master course complete with assessments and assignments that align to the identified learning outcomes. When this master course approach is used, instructors are typically provided a standardized syllabus and are expected to use the predetermined assignments and assessments; however, they are given the flexibility to determine the best teaching methods to use. At some colleges and universities, one lead faculty member or course coordinator may be responsible for designing the course. At other colleges and universities, course design happens at the instructor level.

Institutional practices related to course design obviously apply to the first-year seminar. In other words, it is important for those who are designing or redesigning the course to follow institutional protocol. In many cases, there will be specific forms to complete and different committees or task forces will need to be involved.

There are some unique issues related to this course that should be taken into consideration during the design or redesign process. For starters, many colleges and universities may only have one faculty member dedicated to the first-year seminar course. In some cases, the course coordinator may be an administrator or a student services professional rather than a member of the faculty. This is not typically the case in other disciplines such as business or psychology where there is often a large pool of faculty who are members of a department and have expertise in the subject matter. Because many colleges and universities do not have a first-year seminar department, determining who should participate on the course design team can be a challenge.

It is best when courses are designed by experts in the field. It makes sense that biology faculty members develop biology courses and history faculty members develop history courses. Determining who the first-year seminar experts are can be more challenging. Often faculty from various disciplines such as biology and history teach the course, even if they do not have a strong background in the first-year experience field. While graduate programs in the first-year experience do exist, it is not commonplace for instructors to have this background.

Although it is often advantageous to have faculty from a variety of disciplines teaching the course, especially if a college or university is using an academic program or major-themed approach to the course, it is critical that the course is designed by faculty and professionals who have expertise in the curriculum content of first-year seminars. Sometimes this will include faculty from other disciplines who have taught this course for a number of years and who have participated in extensive professional development on the first-year seminar. If this is not the case, it is probably best to invite other faculty from different disciplines to teach the first-year seminar course after it has been designed.

Another challenge is that the first-year seminar course is often taught by part-time faculty. Although some colleges and universities include part-time faculty in the course design process, it is more typical for full-time faculty to be the key players in the course design process. When it comes to designing the first-year seminar course, it can be very helpful to include part-time faculty in the process. This is especially true at colleges and universities where there is only one full-time faculty member involved in the course. However, part-time faculty may not have the time to commit to this work, especially if they are employed full-time elsewhere or are teaching at several different institutions. Another challenge may be related to financial incentives. There may not be a compensation structure in place, or the funds to implement such a process, to incentivize the participation of part-time faculty in the course design process. Course design and redesign is a complex process that is quite time-consuming.

Given the nature of the first-year seminar course, it may be very helpful to include experts from student affairs, who may not typically be involved in designing academic courses. The curriculum of the first-year seminar often includes content that is both academic and student-affairs focused. Keup and Petschauer (2011) note that student services professionals often have a strong background in student development theory that can be incredibly beneficial in the course design process. Thus, looking for experts from across the institution to participate on the course design team is recommended. For example, involving professionals from the library, advising and counseling departments, and the tutoring center can add value to the process.

The director of the teaching and learning center or others who are responsible for professional development could be great members of the course design team. Teaching and learning center directors often have strong pedagogical expertise in the area of course design and an in-depth knowledge of effective teaching practices. Thus, it can be very helpful to include a professional development specialist on the first-year seminar course design team.

Establishing a core team of experts to design the first-year seminar course is one of the first considerations in the course design process. In some cases, it can be very helpful to have both a small core team and a larger advisory team. If using this approach, the core team can be responsible for designing the course but throughout the process, the core team can gather input from the larger advisory team. Although many professionals may be involved and committed to the course, it is critical that the experts in the content of first-year seminar are the ones designing the course. There is an enormous body of research on student success and those most familiar with this research are the ones best suited to design an effective first-year seminar course.

LEARNING OUTCOMES FOR THE FIRST-YEAR SEMINAR

Once a course design team has been identified to design or redesign the first-year seminar, the team should begin by focusing on the overall purpose of the course and how the first-year seminar course fits into the overall institutional goals. Considering the institutional mission and goals, strategic plan, and how this course can support the mission and goals of the college or university is an important first step.

Student persistence and completion are often top priorities for the institution and the research on the first-year seminar demonstrates that this course can be an integral part of institutional retention and success efforts (Karp & Stacey, 2013). Given that there are numerous ways to increase student persistence and get students to the finish line, it is important to take a closer look at institutional values, challenges, and assessment data to determine the focus of the first-year seminar. For instance, the first-year seminar course can focus on building academic skills if academic readiness is an issue and priority for the college or university. Likewise, building stronger connections with peers, faculty, and staff can be a focus of first-year seminars at institutions where students are indicating a low sense of belonging.

According to the National Resource Center on The First-Year Experience and Students in Transition, there are several different types of first-year seminars (Young & Hopp, 2014). Historically, the extended orientation approach to the course has been the most widely used one across institutions, but academic-focused courses have been significantly increasing in popularity (Keup & Petschauer, 2011). Extended orientation approaches to the course typically focus on assisting students with the transition to college and emphasize connection to the institution. Academically focused first-year seminars, on the other hand, focus on building study skills or introducing students to a specific discipline. The nature of the first-year seminar will likely depend on the institutional values and challenges.

Colleges and universities committed to the Guided Pathways movement described by Bailey et al. (2015) will have institutional goals related to helping students choose and stay on a path. If this is the case, the first-year seminar course will likely have an academic planning and career focus. More specifically, engaging in career exploration and decision making, developing an educational plan, determining what learning strategies work best, and becoming more resilient and gritty could be the primary themes of the first-year seminar course. See appendix B for a first-year seminar sample syllabus that was developed to align with Guided Pathways.

After considering the institutional goals and priorities, the course design team can determine the course learning outcomes. As Wiggins and McTighe (2005) emphasize, learning outcomes are the first consideration in backward design. The course design team will need to determine approximately three to five learning outcomes that capture the primary purpose of the course.

Historically, the three most frequently identified learning outcomes have centered on helping students develop a connection with the institution, familiarizing students with campus resources and services, and assisting students with developing academic skills (Young & Hopp, 2014). However, there are numerous other learning outcomes that are often addressed in this course. Keup and Petschauer (2011) note that most first-year seminars focus learning outcomes on the following areas: academic skills, campus connection, interpersonal skills, personal development, and citizenship. One area that is glaringly missing is career exploration and planning. Unfortunately, career exploration is not typically a key focus in first-year seminars.

In 2017, the first-year seminar course coordinators from New Jersey community colleges met to discuss reimagining the first-year seminar course to align with Guided Pathways. Course coordinators were challenged to rethink the learning outcomes for the first-year seminar so that this course could better help students choose and stay on a pathway. As a result of these statewide meetings, the course coordinators identified the following set of learning outcomes (Center for Student Success at New Jersey Council of County Colleges, n.d.).

Students will develop a higher sense of self-efficacy by doing the following:

1. Identifying and utilizing strategies and resources that promote academic success, personal growth, and resilience
2. Demonstrating critical thinking, information literacy, and technological skills
3. Practicing interpersonal and leadership skills essential in a diverse, global society

4. Reflecting on values, goals, decisions, and actions in relation to the impact on self and others
5. Creating academic, career, and financial plans

COURSE CONTENT

After learning outcomes are established, the course design team can turn their attention to the specific topics that will be addressed in the course. According to national survey data, the most frequently cited topics for the first-year seminar are campus resources, academic planning, and critical thinking (Young & Hopp, 2014). Some additional common first-year seminar topics include goal setting, time management, financial literacy, intercultural competence, written and oral communication, information literacy, and motivation. As previously discussed, career exploration and planning is also an important topic, especially within the Guided Pathways framework.

As you can imagine, it can be quite easy to create a long list of topics to teach in the first-year seminar. To complicate matters, coordinators of the first-year seminar course are often approached by others at their institution about including additional curriculum content. For example, the first-year seminar course can become the place where mandated trainings on topics such as drug and alcohol awareness and sexual harassment are addressed. However, having too many topics or content areas can be problematic.

As noted by Bailey et al. (2015), first-year seminars that address numerous goals and topics often do so in a superficial way that does not lead to long-lasting learning or behavior changes that lead to success. It is therefore important for colleges and universities to spend some time thinking about the priority learning outcomes and content areas for the first-year seminar. To be most effective, the first-year seminar needs to be focused on key learning goals and content areas, not address an endless list of topics related to student success. As an example, the New Jersey first-year seminar course coordinators decided on the following topics (Center for Student Success at New Jersey Council of County Colleges, n.d.):

- Career exploration and academic planning
- Purpose and structure of higher education
- Goal setting
- Decision making, critical thinking, and information literacy
- Grit and resilience
- Self-reflection
- Study strategies
- Financial literacy

ASSESSING FIRST-YEAR SEMINAR LEARNING OUTCOMES

After learning outcomes are identified, the next step in the course design process is to determine what assessments will provide evidence that students have successfully achieved the course learning outcomes (Wiggins & McTighe, 2005). This involves identifying final products that illustrate knowledge and skills learned by students throughout the semester. Some commonly used summative assessments are final exams, papers, or projects. Summative assessments are assignments that are typically completed at the end of the semester, as they are designed to assess what was learned during the semester (Wininger, 2005). Walvoord and Anderson (1998) remind us of the importance of developing assignments that challenge and interest students and that are "likely to elicit from your students the kind of learning you want to measure" (p. 22).

Summative assessments need to address the entire set of course learning outcomes. It is important to note, however, that it is not necessary to identify one summative assessment for each learning outcome. Rather, it is often possible to identify a summative assessment that can show evidence of multiple learning outcomes. For example, if students are asked to complete an in-depth career portfolio project, this assignment could address several learning outcomes. Using the course learning outcomes identified by New Jersey community college course coordinators as an example, this type of summative project could potentially address all the outcomes identified. Similarly, requiring students to work in a group to do a presentation on a research study related to student success can address the first four learning outcomes identified by New Jersey community college first-year seminar course coordinators.

Additional summative assessments will be necessary if one assignment doesn't fully address every course learning outcome. However, it's not productive to have too many summative assignments. The course design team can aim to identify just a couple of major summative assignments that align to the course learning outcomes. A focused curriculum sets the stage for deeper learning (Bailey et al., 2015).

There are typically several appropriate summative assessments that can align well to course learning outcomes. In other words, there isn't one perfect assignment, but rather there are several different assignments that could show evidence of successful completion of the identified learning outcomes. Svinicki and McKeachie (2014) suggest giving students a choice about assignments, if all the options will show evidence of the identified learning outcomes. For example, perhaps students can choose whether they will write a paper, deliver a presentation, or create a website that summarizes research on a student success topic. Incorporating choice into the course design can increase student motivation and give students an opportunity to use their creativity to meet the learning outcomes for the course (Wlodkowski, 2008).

After the major summative assignments have been identified, the course design team can determine what formative assessments are needed. Formative assessments are designed to be learning opportunities that build the knowledge and skills needed for success on summative assessments (Wininger, 2005). When determining which formative assessments will work best, the course design team can think about what content knowledge and skills are needed for students to successfully complete the major assignments. For example, if the summative assignment is to write a paper, the formative assessments could be to identify appropriate sources for the paper and to develop an organizational plan using an outline or concept map. Similarly, if the summative assignment is a presentation, an example of a formative assessment could be a draft of the PowerPoint slides. Quizzes would be considered formative assessments that are linked to exams.

A well-designed course will have several formative assessments for each summative assessment (Harrington & Thomas, 2018). When creating formative and summative assessments, it is important to keep in mind that the purpose of each type of assessment is different. Although all assignments are learning opportunities, learning is the primary focus of formative assessments. The primary focus of summative assessments, on the other hand, is to demonstrate what has been learned. Examples of summative and formative assessments and assignments can be found in the Sample Syllabus (appendix B). It is best when students see the connection between formative and summative assessments rather than just viewing the assignments as a list of "to-do" items. This approach can increase value and meaning for students. Too often, students are asked to do numerous isolated tasks in a first-year seminar course rather than tasks that are aligned to the learning outcomes and major, summative assignments.

Feedback plays an incredibly powerful role in the learning process (Nicol & Macfarlane-Dick, 2006; Taras, 2006). Linking formative assessments to summative assessments can increase the likelihood that students will meet with success because this approach gives students the opportunity to use feedback to improve on upcoming, related tasks or assignments. For example, having students do a paper on the same topic as a group presentation gives students the opportunity to take the feedback received from the paper and use it to create a strong presentation. This approach can also increase group productivity. Research has found that student groups function more effectively if students are required to first complete an individual assignment related to the group project (Sarfo & Elen, 2011).

ENSURING LEARNING: TEACHING METHODS

Determining which teaching methods will best help students successfully achieve the course learning outcomes is the next step in the backward design process (Wiggins & McTighe, 2005). Teaching methods refer to in and out of class activities that are used to facilitate learning. Some frequently used teaching methods include the lecture, discussion, group work, and experiential learning activities. Although the course design team may share teaching strategy suggestions, instructors typically have the academic freedom to determine which teaching methods will work best. Thus, this part of the process is most commonly designed at the instructor level.

First-year seminar instructors will want to think about teaching methods on both a broad course level and from a more specific class level. Thus, although a first-year seminar instructor may decide to use interactive lectures and group work throughout the semester, instructors will need to determine when to use each approach. The specific teaching method will likely vary from class to class across the semester depending on the class-level learning objectives.

Class-level learning objectives, the goals for each particular class, can be used to determine which teaching method will be most effective. For example, if the objective for the class is for students to be able to identify and evaluate sources of information for academic products such as papers or presentations, an effective teaching approach could be a brief lecture and demonstration followed by an opportunity for students to search and evaluate sources during class while the instructor is present and able to act as a helpful resource. Perhaps a librarian could even be a guest in the class that day to provide support as needed.

If, on the other hand, a learning objective is focused on developing interpersonal skills, some type of collaborative group work or an experiential opportunity such as a field experience would probably work best. Often a combination of different teaching methods will be used in each class period. The key is for instructors to be intentional and planful about which teaching strategies to use and when in order to help students achieve the course learning outcomes.

Regardless of the specific teaching method, instructors' familiarity with pedagogical theory and research will prove useful in the course design process. For example, instructors can be guided by the seminal work of Chickering and Gamson (1987). Chickering and Gamson (1987) encourage faculty to use teaching methods that align to the following seven effective practices:

- Strong student-faculty relationships
- Cooperative learning experiences
- Active learning opportunities

- Prompt, frequent feedback
- Tasks that require time and effort
- Having and communicating high expectations
- Providing a variety of ways for diverse learners to demonstrate success

As first-year seminar instructors consider which teaching methods to use, it can be helpful to focus on these guiding principles. When instructors choose teaching methods that focus on the end goal of learning and are aligned to guiding principles of effective teaching practices, higher levels of student achievement are more likely.

Although several different teaching approaches can successfully help students achieve the desired objectives or outcomes, some teaching methods will work better than others for different purposes. It is therefore important for instructors to focus on the goal or outcome and the best way to achieve that goal. For example, if one of the course learning outcomes is focused on building critical thinking skills, discussions can be an effective teaching approach. However, research has shown that online discussions, as compared to in-person discussions, are often more likely to result in higher-level critical thinking skills (Guiller, Durndell, & Ross, 2008).

Online discussions allow students to review materials and think deeply about the question posed prior to posting their contribution. Instructors may therefore want to use online discussions to supplement in-class discussions or even shift discussions from the classroom to the online environment. Instructors will want to consider the evidence behind different teaching strategies so that they can choose the ones that will work best for the specific goals of each class.

It is also important to consider the student body when selecting a teaching method. Research has shown that some teaching methods are more effective for novice learners, while others are more effective for those with a higher level of expertise. For example, Clark, Kircshner, and Sweller (2012) found that direct instruction, otherwise known as the lecturing teaching method, is most helpful to novice or new learners.

Lee and Anderson (2013) noted that the opposite was true for experts. Although experts can certainly learn from lectures, they learned best when given the opportunity to engage in group work. Lee and Anderson (2013) call this the expertise reversal effect. It is therefore important for instructors to consider the background knowledge their students have in the subject matter. Instructors may want to use the lecturing teaching method more frequently when the students in their classes do not yet know much about the discipline and increase group work as knowledge increases.

After a teaching method has been identified, instructors can turn their attention to determining how to best implement the teaching method selected. Any teaching method, if not utilized effectively, can be ineffective.

For examples, lectures have often been viewed as passive and ineffective (Freeman et al., 2014). However, Harrington and Zakrajsek (2017) show strong evidence that the lecturing technique can be effective, especially when used in combination with brief, interactive opportunities. For example, researchers have found that giving students several two-minute purposeful pauses, where students discuss their notes with a classmate, lead to higher levels of learning (Bachhel & Thaman, 2014; Ruhl, Hughes, & Schloss, 1987). Incorporating brief opportunities for students to process and reflect on content learned increases the effectiveness of lecturing as a teaching method.

Given the personal nature and skill-based focus of the first-year seminar, it is not surprising that active learning approaches are frequently used. Effective use of active pedagogical practices has been noted as one of the reasons for positive outcomes associated with the first-year seminar course (Friedman, 2017). In fact, collaborative assignments and projects was the most frequently cited high-impact practice in first-year seminars (Young & Hopp, 2014).

Group work can be used to help students build long-lasting knowledge, develop skills, and engage in critical thinking. "Cooperative learning is founded on a deep historical research base, with new research on how people learn and on deep learning providing added insights into its efficacy" (Millis, 2010, p. 2). Using groups as a teaching method can help students achieve learning outcomes related to course content and can also facilitate effective peer relationships, enhancing student support systems and increasing resilience.

Like the lecture method, group work also needs to be carefully designed in order to have positive outcomes. To increase productivity and the effectiveness of the group, instructors can consider ways to foster interdependence and individual accountability (Millis, 2002). In other words, well-designed group work requires students to work together to successfully complete the task and is planned in such a way that all members must actively participate. Nilson (2016) suggests teaching students how to successfully participate in a group project, as this approach has been found to increase productivity and performance.

To summarize, instructors need to consider many factors when deciding which teaching method to use. Most importantly, the learning outcome or objective should be the primary consideration. Different teaching methods will work best for different learning goals. In addition, the students and their background knowledge need to be considered. After a teaching method has been identified, instructors will want to investigate the best way to effectively implement that approach.

SEQUENCING: THE COURSE OUTLINE

After determining the outcomes, assessments, and teaching methods, first-year instructors can shift their attention to sequencing the learning tasks. Traditionally, many instructors have used the required textbook for the course to guide the sequencing of course content delivery. In other words, chapter 1 content becomes the focus of week 1, chapter 2 for week 2, and so forth. However, Wiggins and McTighe (2005) advocate for sequencing course content in a way that best supports students performing well on the identified assessments. In the backward design approach, the textbook can serve as an important course resource but does not play a primary role in determining the course outline.

To develop the course outline using backward design, first-year seminar instructors can decide when the major projects or assessments should be due. For example, in a course where there are two major assignments—perhaps one with a career focus and another with an academic focus—instructors can determine if both major assignments will be due toward the end of the semester or if one will be due around the mid-point of the semester and the other at the end of the semester. Once the major assignments are listed on the course outline, the first-year seminar instructor can then work backward to determine when the formative assessments or assignments that align to each major project will be due. All of these due dates can be documented in the course outline.

Next, instructors need to think about how the sequencing of content and identified teaching methods can support student success on these formative and summative assessments. In a backward design approach, many of the course topics may be revisited as needed to support student learning. For example, instead of time management being taught as a stand-alone, isolated lesson that corresponds to the textbook sequence, time-management can be addressed at multiple points throughout the semester, especially when these skills are needed to complete a project successfully. Students can be encouraged to revisit that section of the text as needed. To see an example of how the backward design course outline differs from a traditionally sequenced outline, see the Sample Syllabus (appendix B).

THE SYLLABUS

The syllabus can be used as a vehicle to share the course learning outcomes and the overall design of the course with students. Students will turn to the syllabus to understand the purpose and expectations of the course. In addition to being an informational document, the syllabus can also be used as a motivational tool that gets students excited about the course. This is particularly likely when the syllabus clearly communicates the learning goals and the path that students will need to take in order to meet with success (Harrington & Thomas, 2018).

When using a backward design approach, one of the most important communication considerations is helping students see the connection between assignments and the course learning outcomes. According to Palmer (2017), student motivation and engagement are higher when faculty clearly articulate expectations, the rationale behind assignments, and show how assignments will help students accomplish the learning goals for the course. Although the connection and meaning among and between assignments may be obvious to you as the instructor, this may not be the case for students. It is therefore very helpful to explicitly make these connections via the syllabus.

Learning outcomes should take center stage on the syllabus, especially in a course that is developed using backward design. Unfortunately, research has shown that students often have difficulty recalling the course learning outcomes after reviewing syllabi (Smith & Razzouk, 1993). To combat this issue, instructors can use visual tools such as graphics, images, or color to draw attention to the course learning outcomes and can review these learning outcomes during class (Harrington & Thomas, 2018).

In addition, instructors can describe how assignments are linked to learning outcomes. There are several ways that instructors can make these links explicit. One approach is to provide a rationale for each assignment, explaining the purpose of the assignment and clearly describing how each assignment is designed to help students achieve the course learning outcomes. Another approach is to list learning outcomes after each assignment, and yet another approach is to develop a table that illustrates the connection. Using visual tools to package course content and demonstrate connections can be helpful (Sauer & Calimeris, 2015).

Many institutions use a master syllabus for the first-year seminar. A master syllabus is particularly helpful at colleges and universities that have developed learning outcomes and assignments at the department or state level. Even when instructors are provided with a master syllabus, it is important for instructors to personalize this document. Students appreciate knowing information about their instructor. Including an image, brief biographical information, and a teaching philosophy statement can help students feel connected to their instructor. Whether a syllabus is developed at the department, state, or instructor level, using research-based syllabus design practices will increase the likelihood that students use and benefit from this important document (Harrington & Thomas, 2018).

In summary, it is time for colleges and universities to reflect on how the first-year seminar course can best support institutional goals and align to Guided Pathways. Reimagining the first-year seminar using a Guided Pathways framework will likely lead to learning outcomes that focus on career exploration and decision making, academic planning, study strategies, and resiliency. The course design team or course coordinator can use the backward design approach to course design to develop a robust first-year seminar course that will help students choose and stay on a path.

REFERENCES

Anderson, L., & Krathwohl, D. A. (2001). *Taxonomy for learning, teaching, and assessing: A revision of Bloom's taxonomy of educational objectives.* New York, NY: Longman.

Armbruster, P., Patel, M., Johnson, E., & Weiss, M. (2009). Active learning and student-centered pedagogy improve student attitudes and performance in introductory biology. *CBE Life Sciences Education, 8*(3), 203–213.

Bachhel, R. & Thaman, R. G. (2014). Effective use of pause procedure to enhance student engagement and learning. *Journal of Clinical & Diagnostic Research, 8*(8), 1–3. doi:10.7860/JCDR/2014/8260.4691

Bailey, T. R., Smith Jaggars, S., & Jenkins, D. (2015). *Redesigning America's community colleges: A clearer path to student success.* Cambridge, MA. Harvard University Press.

Center for Student Success at the New Jersey Council of County Colleges (n.d.). *Student success course.* Retrieved from https://www.njstudentsuccess.org/student-success-course

Chickering, A. W., and Gamson, Z. F. Seven principles for good practice in undergraduate education. *AAHE Bulletin, 1987, 39*(7), 3–7. Retrieved from http://www.aahea.org/articles/sevenprinciples1987.htm

Clark, R. E., Kircshner, P. A., & Sweller, J. (2012). Putting students on the path to learning: The case for fully guided instruction. *American Educator, 36*(1), 6–11.

Freeman, S., Eddy, S. L., McDonough, M., Smith, M. K., Okoroafor, N., Jordt, H., & Wenderoth, M. P. (2014). Active learning increases student performance in science, engineering, and mathematics. *Proceedings of the National Academy of Sciences, 111*(23), 8410–8415. Retrieved from http://www.pnas.org/content/111/23/8410

Friedman, D. (2017, December). *First-year experience: Engaging students through active learning.* Presented at the New Jersey Center for Student Success, Edison, NJ.

Grocia, J. E., & Hunter, M. S. (2012). *The first-year seminar: Designing, implementing, and assessing courses to support student learning and success: Vol. II. Instructor training and development.* Columbia, SC: University of South Carolina, National Resource Center for The First-Year Experience and Students in Transition.

Guiller, J., Durndell, A., & Ross, A. (2008). Peer interaction and critical thinking: Face-to-face or online discussion? *Learning & Instruction, 18*(2), 187–200. doi:10.1016/j.learninstruc.2007.03.001

Haras, C., Taylor, S. C., Sorcinelli, M. D., & von Hoene, L. (2017). *Institutional commitment to teaching excellence: Assessing the impacts and outcomes of faculty development.* Washington DC: American Council on Education.

Harrington, C., & Thomas, M. (2018). *Designing a motivational syllabus: Creating a learning path for student engagement.* Sterling, VA: Stylus.

Harrington, C., & Zakrajsek, T. (2017). *Dynamic lecturing: Research-based strategies to enhance lecture effectiveness.* Sterling, VA: Stylus.

Karp, M. M., & Stacey, G. W. (2013). What we know about nonacademic student supports. *Community College Research Center, Teachers College, Columbia University.* Retrieved from https://ccrc.tc.columbia.edu/publications/what-we-know-student-supports.html

Keup, J. R., & Petschauer, J. W. (2011). *The first-year seminar: Designing, implementing, and assessing courses to support student learning and success: Vol 1: Designing and administering the course.* Columbia, SC: University of South Carolina. National Resource Center for the First-Year Experience and Students in Transition.

Lee, H. S., & Anderson J. R. (2013). Student learning: What's instruction got to do with it? *Annual Review Psychology, 64,* 445–469.

Levine, L. E., Fallahi, C. R., Nicoll-Senft, J. M., Tessier, J. T., Watson, C. L., & Wood, R. M. (2008). Creating significant learning experiences across disciplines. *College Teaching, 56*(4), 247–254.

Millis, B. J. (2002). Enhancing learning—and more! Through cooperative learning. IDEA Paper #38. Retrieved from https://www.ideaedu.org/Portals/0/Uploads/Documents/ IDEA%20Papers/IDEA%20Papers/IDEA_Paper_38.pdf

Millis, B. J. (2010). *Cooperative learning in higher education.* Sterling, VA: Stylus.

Nicol, D. J., & Macfarlane-Dick, D. (2006). Formative assessment and self-regulated learning: A model and seven principles of good feedback practice. *Studies in Higher Education, 31*(2), 199–218.

Nilson, L. B. (2016). *Teaching at its best: A research-based resource for college instructors.* San Francisco, CA: Jossey-Bass.

Palmer, M. S. (2017, June). *The science of transparency.* Plenary presentation at the Lilly Teaching and Learning Conference, Bethesda, MD.

Reynolds, H. L., & Kearns, K. D. (2017). A planning tool for incorporating backward design, active learning, and authentic assessment in the college classroom. *College Teaching, 65*(1), 17–27.

Rienties, B., & Toetenel, L. (2016). The impact of learning design on student behaviour, satisfaction and performance: A cross-institutional comparison across 151 modules. *Computers in Human Behavior, 60*, 333–341. doi:10.1016/j.chb.2016.02.074

Ruhl, K., Hughes, C., and Schloss, P. (1987). Using the pause procedure to enhance lecture recall. *Teacher Education and Special Education*, 10, 14–18.

Sarfo, F., & Elen, J. (2011). Investigating the impact of positive resource interdependence and individual accountability on students' academic performance in cooperative learning. *Electronic Journal of Research in Educational Psychology, 9*(1), 73–93.

Sauer, K. M., & Calimeris, L. (2015). The syllabus evolved: Extended graphic syllabi for Economics courses. *Journal of Economics and Economic Education Research, 16*(1), 135–148.

Smith, M. F., & Razzouk, N. Y. (1993). Improving classroom communication: The case of the course syllabus. *Journal of Education for Business, 68*(4), 215–222. Retrieved from Academic Search Premiere.

Svinicki, M. D., & McKeachie, W. J. (2014*). McKeachie's teaching tips: Strategies, research, and theory for college and university teachers.* 14th ed. Belmont, CA: Wadsworth, Cengage Learning.

Taras, M. (2006). Do unto others or not: Equity in feedback for undergraduate. *Assessment and Evaluation in Higher Education, 31*(3), 365–377.

Walvoord, B. E., & Anderson, V. J. (1998). Effective grading: A tool for learning and assessment. San Francisco, CA: Jossey Bass.

Wang, X., Su, Y., Cheung, S., Wong, E., & Kwong, T. (2013). An exploration of Biggs' constructive alignment in course design and its impact on students' learning approaches. *Assessment and Evaluation in Higher Education, 38*(4), 477–491. doi:10.1080/ 02602938.2012.658018

Wiggins, G., & McTighe, J. (2005). *Understanding by design* (expanded 2nd ed.). Upper Saddle River, NJ: Pearson.

Wininger, S. R. (2005). Using your tests to teach: Formative summative assessment. *Teaching of Psychology, 32*(3), 164–166. doi:10.1207/s15328023top3203_7

Winkelmes, M., Bernacki, M., Butler, J., Zochowski, M., Golanics, J., & Weavil, K. H. (2016). A teaching intervention that increases underserved college students' success. *Peer Review, 18*(1–2), 31–36.

Wlodkowski, R. J. (2008). *Enhancing adult motivation to learn: A comprehensive guide for teaching all adults* (3rd ed.). San Francisco, CA: Jossey-Bass.

Young, D. G., & Hopp, J. M. (2014). *2012–2013 National Survey of First-Year Seminars: Exploring high impact practices in the first college year* (Research Report No. 4). Columbia, SC: University of South Carolina, National Resource Center for The First-Year Experience and Students in Transition.

Chapter Six

Being Your Campus Champion

*A Three-Credit Mandatory First-Year Seminar Course
for All Students*

Once the first-year seminar has been redesigned to align to Guided Pathways, first-year seminar course coordinators need to champion the course so that it can be included in academic programs. Based on the research on the first-year seminar, all first-year students should be required to take the course. This is already common practice at many colleges and universities. According to the results of a 2012–2013 national survey, 42.5% of colleges and universities reported requiring the course of all students (Young & Hopp, 2014). Many other colleges and universities require the first-year seminar course of most students as indicated by 55.9% of institutions responding to this same survey reporting that the course is required of 90% or more of incoming first-year students.

However, there are still many colleges and universities that are not requiring this course or only requiring the course for a small percentage of first-year students. Unfortunately, 31.1% of two-year colleges required fewer than 10% of their incoming students to take the course. This number is 18.7% at four-year colleges. Thus, four-year colleges are more likely to require first-semester students to take the first-year seminar course. Private institutions were also more likely to require the course as compared to public institutions (Young & Hopp, 2014).

As a result, many students, especially students at community colleges, are missing out on the benefits of the first-year seminar course. Given the incredibly strong data that connect this course to numerous positive student outcomes such as increased retention and graduation rates, this finding is quite problematic. The Guided Pathways movement that has grown out of the community college sector—but is also highly relevant to four-year colleges and universities—is about increasing student success rates for all students (Bailey, Jaggars, & Jenkins, 2015). After reviewing the effectiveness of various institutional initiatives at numerous colleges, Jenkins (2014) concluded that pilots to scale simply do not work. Unfortunately, institutions that created programs or services for small groups of students didn't see increases in retention and graduation rates. Thus, Jenkins (2014) strongly advocates for changes at scale. This means that colleges and universities should put their time and energy into redesigning services and supports that reach all students.

WHY EVERYONE? AN EQUITY ISSUE

According to the most recent triennial National Survey of First-Year Seminars, the top three categories of first-year seminar course enrollees were academically underprepared students, students in specific majors, and students enrolled in remedial or developmental courses (Young & Hopp, 2014). At public and two-year institutions, which were less likely to require students to take the course, most of the students enrolled in the course were largely academically unprepared or enrolled in developmental/remedial courses. At public institutions in particular, first-year seminar students were also more likely to be enrolled in learning communities or support programs such as the federal TRIO program. A majority of the survey participants indicated that they offered at least one special section of the course. Close to one in six institutions reported offering a special section for academically underprepared students. By contrast 25% of four-year institutions reported offering a special section for honors students (Young & Hopp, 2014).

Research has clearly shown that the first-year seminar benefits all students. However, the students who benefit the most are those who are considered academically underprepared or at risk for other reasons. Students with lower levels of academic achievement significantly benefit from working with peers who have stronger academic backgrounds. In addition, the mindset of students taking a course required of all students is very different from another requirement because of a placement test score. In the latter situation, students will quickly develop a lower sense of self-efficacy for college, which will not serve them well. Instead, being in a course that is required of all students sends the message that all students belong and need to be supported during this transitional period.

These survey results challenge the stereotypical view of the course. The first-year seminar course is typically thought of as a course for academically unprepared students at community colleges and broad-access public four-year institutions. What these survey results show is that far more private institutions require the course, with nearly one-quarter of them offering a section for high-achieving students (Young & Hopp, 2014). In other words, the students who may need the course the most are often not the ones who are required to take the first-year seminar course.

"In most institutions of higher education, the discourse of deficit and diversity are more likely to be heard than the discourse of equity. But the kinds of personal and institutional changes needed to eliminate the achievement gap are more likely to originate from equity thinking" (Bensimon, 2005, p. 104). Guided Pathways is based on an equity mindset. Its overarching goal is to improve persistence and completion rates for all college students, regardless of their academic preparedness.

Given their long-standing collegiate history, first-year seminar courses are ideally situated to play a pivotal role in the Guided Pathways movement; however, for that to occur conversations concerning first-year seminar courses must also be based on equity thinking. Too often first-year seminar courses are viewed as punitive—mandated because of a student's poor performance on a college placement test. This is an example of the deficit mindset that has dominated much of the discussion concerning retention, persistence, and remedial courses. For the students who must take the course because they placed into remedial coursework, it sends the message that the college or university does not believe in their ability to be successful.

It is true that many college policies surrounding remedial coursework and the first-year seminar often stem from a place of support, with college faculty and staff wanting to help students build skills so that they can meet with success. Unfortunately, the data are not supporting these approaches.

Developmental education has been found to be one of the biggest roadblocks to success. Research has found that full-time undergraduate students who take remedial courses in their first year of college are 74% more likely to drop out of college and students who persist take 11 more months to graduate (Barry and Dannenberg, 2016). Over 60% of incoming community college students place into at least one developmental education course but only 20% of these students complete any college-level course within three years (Couturier and Cullinane, 2015).

Likewise, research has shown that the least effective type of first-year seminar is the one that is only required of at-risk students (Permzadian & Crede, 2016). These findings were based on a meta-analysis of first-year students. Results also revealed that first-year seminars were much more successful when all students were required to take the course (Permzadian & Crede, 2016).

Imagine the potential for this course if it is required of all students and has a robust curriculum. Even though many institutions are only requiring this course of underprepared students who are enrolled in developmental or remedial courses, results of research have still been overwhelmingly positive. If colleges and universities shift their approach and instead require all students to take the course, successful outcomes will likely soar higher. Current findings, while positive, may not tell the whole story. More meaningful data would result from studies at colleges and universities that require a first-year seminar course of all students and a curriculum aligned to Guided Pathways.

First-year seminar courses offer the possibility of impacting long-term student outcomes if they are part of a well-conceived Guided Pathways plan. An institution's implementation plan should entail an initial assessment of all its existing resources to determine which of them need no revision, some revision, or a complete redesign. Like any long-standing course, first-year seminar courses will likely need some revisions to more closely align with the principles of Guided Pathways.

Research has been conducted to better understand how first-year seminar courses can be revised to improve their impact on long-term student outcomes. Two studies by the Community College Research Center (CCRC) at Columbia University have yielded some important insights. Using a theory of action, they better explained why first-year seminar courses should improve long-term student outcomes. Karp et al. (2012) investigated the implementation of a standardized first-year seminar course at three community colleges within the Virginia state system.

The researchers dismissed the common assumption that helping students develop campus connections and an awareness of college resources in the first-year seminar would lead to student integration and persistence; instead they suggested that long-term outcomes would be realized only when students applied their course-acquired skills and knowledge. For this to occur, they maintained, the course had to focus on teaching-for-application rather than information dissemination. Students needed to be introduced to new knowledge about academic success skills and campus resources, become aware of how and when to use these skills and resources, and develop the initiative and motivation to use the skills and resources. This would occur when opportunities for applied learning, contextualization, reflection, and deliberate practice were incorporated into the curriculum.

Karp, Raufman, Efthimiou, and Ritze (2015) studied Bronx Community College's first-year seminar course. Their findings illustrated how the course was successfully restructured to positively influence long-term outcomes. Like much of the research on first-year seminars, this study also found that the short-term outcomes of students who took the course were better than those who had not.

First-year seminar students had higher first-semester grade point averages and earned, on average, more credits in their first semester than students who had not taken the course. The good news is that these findings showed that these early gains continued over time. After two years, first-year seminar students maintained higher grade point averages than their non-first-year seminar counterparts and their one-year retention rate was nearly 10 percentage points higher when compared to non-first-year seminar students. The researchers attributed these long-term outcomes to three emphases within the curriculum: introduction to key skills and knowledge, opportunities for practice and reflection, and application of first-year seminar knowledge to new situations (Karp et al., 2015).

Students reported that they were able to practice their newly acquired skills and knowledge during mandated meetings with academic advisors, library visits, and hands-on classroom activities. In subsequent semester interviews, students reported continued use of their first-year seminar acquired skills through ongoing interactions with their academic advisors, utilization of the library's database, and regular communication with their professors.

These studies emphasize the importance of providing students with the chance to practice the student success skills that are introduced in the first-year seminar course. Utilizing a Guided Pathways approach in the course can offer students a variety of ways in which this can be accomplished. From regular assessment of their academic and career plans, to meeting with an advisor to ensure they are on track to meet their graduation or transfer goals, Guided Pathways' principles can be integrated into the course in ways that contextualize course material and provide regular opportunities for discussion, reflection, and application of the success strategies that are an integral component of the first-year seminar.

There are signs that the mindset about how to best support students is changing. With the growing popularity of accelerated learning programs, as well as the corequisite remediation approach to developmental education, the shift toward equity thinking has begun. Discussions are not about which remedial courses students place into but rather which remedial courses they place out of.

At many colleges and universities, students no longer spend multiple semesters in remediation. Instead, corequisite support classes allow them to concurrently enroll in credit-bearing, college-level courses. This is an incredibly positive shift. The data show that this corequisite approach is effective. In states where corequisite remediation initiatives have been enacted systemwide, the results have found that students enrolled in one-semester corequisite English courses typically succeeded at twice the rate of students enrolled in traditional prerequisite English courses. Similarly, the success rates of students enrolled in gateway mathematics courses that were aligned with their major were five to six times that of students who were enrolled in traditional remedial mathematics sequences (Vandal, 2015).

Unfortunately, this positive approach to developmental education has caused a drop in first-year seminar course enrollment at institutions where the seminar is tied to remedial courses. This means that fewer students are benefiting from the first-year seminar course since it is only required of students taking developmental education courses. This is another reason why institutions need to redefine the role of the first-year seminar course in light of these higher education reform movements.

First-year seminar courses should not be restricted to students who are considered academically at risk or underprepared. The curriculum, especially one aligned to Guided Pathways, is relevant for all new students. It transitions students from their initial on-boarding experience to a course that provides them with the opportunity and resources needed to develop their burgeoning academic and career plans, along with their college readiness skills. The first-year seminar, like other required courses such as English, provides students with essential knowledge and skills needed for success.

The national attention being paid to the Guided Pathways movement provides an ideal opportunity to promote the importance of a three-credit, mandatory first-year seminar course. To do so, it is important to address the deficit thinking that is often associated with the course and stress that the first-year seminar is not a remedial course. The topics that are covered are universal, not developmental, and help all students reach their academic potential. Much in the same way that students in corequisite remedial support classes are bolstered by enrollment in credit-bearing classes with college-ready peers, students in credit-bearing first-year seminar courses benefit from the sharing of myriad ideas and experiences that arise in a classroom setting that is not delineated by a student's level of academic readiness.

Number of Credits

In addition to requiring the course for all students, assigning sufficient credit to the first-year seminar course is imperative to establishing its value and legitimacy. Currently, colleges and universities across the nation offer this course for no credit, one credit, two credits, three credits, or even four or more credits. Most decisions about the number of credits have been made based on issues relating to campus culture rather than based on how much time is needed to achieve the course learning outcomes. For example, a college may have decided on a one- or two-credit course because it was easier to fit one or two credits into already existing curricula and because this approach may have increased the likelihood of having the course approved by the faculty senate or curriculum committee.

In some ways, just having a conversation about the number of credits devalues the course. If all the other courses provide students with three credits, why would this course be different? If colleges and universities are engaged in conversation about how many credits all courses should be, then it makes perfect sense for the first-year seminar course to be included in this conversation. However, if this is the only course that colleges and universities are discussing regarding the number of credits, why is this the case? One of the most frequent complaints of first-year seminar instructors and course coordinators, especially those teaching one- or two-credit versions of the course, is that there is not enough time to achieve the learning outcomes. With a more robust and reimagined course curriculum, this will be even more true.

There is some evidence that supports assigning three credits versus only one or two. At Cincinnati State Technical and Community College, a three-, two-, and one-credit first-year seminar course were compared. Blanton, McLaughlin & Niese (n.d.) found that students preferred the two- and three-credit versions of the course, consistently rating these more favorably than the one-credit version of the course. It is important to note that this trend held true across several years.

Similarly, Jessup-Anger (2011) found that both student and instructor motivation was lower with a one-credit course. This resulted in lower expectations and lower levels of effort, which can obviously be connected to lower levels of academic achievement. Du (2016) reported further evidence for a first-year seminar with more credits. Specifically, at the University of Mount Union, higher levels of retention and student engagement were found after they shifted from a one-credit to four-credit version of the first-year seminar.

Karp et al. (2012) investigated the implementation of a first-year seminar course in a state system. Community colleges were given some autonomy in establishing their courses. The researchers found that the decision by three of the schools to assign one credit to the course had inadvertently devalued it in the eyes of the students and non-first-year seminar staff. It was seen as less important than courses that were awarded three credits. Students did not take the course seriously and instructors who were not associated with the course did not view it as important or useful. Moreover, first-year seminar instructors felt that the one-credit format did not give them enough class time to sufficiently cover the course material. Bailey et al. (2015) caution against only covering topics in the first-year seminar course in a superficial way. Rather, the learning outcomes and course content warrant a significant amount of time on task. Assigning the same number of credits to the first-year seminar as other courses in the curriculum sends an important message about its value and gives students and faculty the time needed to dive deeply into the course content.

Integrating the First-Year Seminar Course into Programs

Establishing a mandatory three-credit first-year seminar course on campus is a massive undertaking that is replete with unforeseen complexities and considerations. This cannot be accomplished without widespread support and a dedicated cross-functional team. Once support is garnered, the challenge of how to integrate the course into programs still exists. There are a variety of ways in which a three-credit first-year seminar course can be integrated into an institution's academic programs. This will be dependent upon internal and external factors such as accreditation requirements, maximum credit limits, and financial aid considerations.

The most expedient approach may be to make the course a graduation requirement for all students, independent of degree programs. However, there will be resistance as some college personnel and students will see this approach as adding more time and money to completion. Questions that will need to be addressed include the following:

- Will financial aid pay for a course that is outside of a student's major?
- What registrar systems need to be in place to ensure that students take the course during their first semester?

It is true that adding course requirements that are not a part of program requirements is antithetical to Guided Pathways. The Guided Pathways approach increases transparency about graduation requirements and encourages colleges and universities to remove requirements that are outside of program requirements.

Thus, requiring the first-year seminar as a graduation requirement that is not integrated into programs is not the ideal way to proceed. However, if getting the course integrated into all programs is not feasible, this graduation requirement approach is significantly better than not requiring the course. Since the goal is student completion, the data on the first-year seminar clearly shows that requiring this course will likely lead to increased success, including higher graduation rates. Thus, the cost-benefit analysis of requiring a course that is not a part of the program suggests that the positives associated with requiring the course outweigh the negatives of it being a requirement outside of the program. When first-year seminar course coordinators are faced with others questioning the value of adding another requirement, the best response is to show the success outcomes for the course. As Cuseo (n.d.a.) noted, on any college campus, the first-year seminar is the course with the most national data indicating its value.

In the community college sector, another question often posed relates to transfer. In other words, critics of the course may question whether the course transfers to four-year colleges and universities. Since four-year colleges are more likely to offer and require this course, as compared to two-year colleges (Young & Hopp, 2014), this does not seem to be an issue of huge concern. However, the world of transfer can be a complex one and there will likely be some colleges or universities that may not accept the first-year seminar for transfer credits. In some cases, this may be because the learning outcomes for the course at the sending and receiving institution are not the same. In other words, the courses may not be similar enough. To combat this issue, it is important for community colleges to understand what is expected of students taking this course at four-year colleges and universities. Then, community colleges will need to communicate the academic rigor of the first-year seminar and the learning outcomes to four-year partners, demonstrating how it aligns to the first-year seminar course offered at their institution.

Perhaps a four-year college or university would be more likelyto accept the first-year seminar with the revised curriculum. It is also important to note that while all efforts should be made to ensure that the first-year seminar course transfers, by requiring this course, it is likely that more students will be graduating and transferring. In other words, even if the credits do not carry over to the four-year school, the chances of graduating and transferring are likely higher because of this course so, again, the cost-benefit analysis seems to favor requiring the course. First-year seminar course coordinators should work closely with transfer partners to ensure that the credits associated with this course do transfer to their institution of their choice; however, the primary value added of the first-year seminar is increased success.

Developing or revising the first-year seminar so that it meets the criteria for general education status is another approach to consider. This approach is a significant improvement from the graduation requirement approach because the course would then be integrated into programs for all students. Given the strong focus a first-year seminar course can have on several general education goals such as critical thinking and information literacy, the first-year seminar is a good fit within the general education structure. Perhaps this is why so many colleges and universities count the course as part of the general education requirements. According to a national survey, 58.6% of colleges reported counting the first-year seminar as a general education requirement (Young & Hopp, 2014). This approach will require participation from faculty who are adept at curriculum development, as well as administrators who have knowledge of internal curriculum approval procedures and external processes at the state-level or system-level that are required for course approval.

The primary advantage of this approach is that institutions will have a credit-bearing general education first-year seminar that can be used within programs to satisfy general education degree requirements. Some colleges and universities may identify a unique category within the structure of general education or may opt to include the first-year seminar as an elective within an already established category such as critical thinking, information literacy, or perhaps even social sciences.

With general education status, the course will be associated with an academic department, which will lend it more academic legitimacy and visibility. As a general education elective, it will also be part of a degree requirement and eligible for financial aid. Thus, if the general education approach is a viable option, it is one worth pursuing.

Another approach is to simply require the first-year seminar in all programs or majors. In other words, the first-year seminar would be a requirement in the same way that general education and major courses are required. To integrate the first-year seminar into the curriculum, this course would likely come from the major or elective categories. In other words, the first-year seminar would replace one of the electives currently in the program.

It can be particularly challenging to garner support from community college faculty for this approach because there are so few major or elective courses in the program. In some cases, requiring the first-year seminar means that the number of major courses could be reduced to just three. While these major or elective courses can provide students with very valuable learning experiences, the national data show that too few students are even getting a chance to benefit from these learning experiences. Strengthening the foundational curriculum with a course such as the first-year seminar can increase the likelihood that students will benefit from the other major and elective courses and complete their degree requirements.

While this approach can work well in many programs, especially those that have many electives, it can be much more challenging in programs with very specific program requirements. Programs with outside accreditors, such as nursing, may be so prescribed that there is no place within the curriculum for the course to reside. Including it in an accredited program may result in exceeding any limits set by the state for maximum credits for degree completion. For programs that do not have to answer to external accrediting bodies, deciding which elective is to be replaced may be cause for debate within academic departments and negatively impact enrollment in other courses, causing dissension in a department. Despite the possible challenges associated with this approach, it is definitely one worth pursuing.

Considering the best approach for including a three-credit mandatory first-year seminar course into an institution's programs will depend upon the institution's culture and resources. It is not a decision to be made lightly as it will prompt much discussion and debate as it will involve numerous constituencies both on and off campus. However, given the strong evidence for this course, it is a conversation that is worth having, as students will be the ones who will benefit if the course can be integrated into the program. First-year seminar course coordinators will need to be ready to provide data to make the case and enlist the support of many others from across campus.

CHAMPIONING THE COURSE TO COLLEAGUES

The purpose behind requiring a three-credit first-year seminar course is to ensure that all students have an equal opportunity to achieve their education and career goals. Making the case for the course will likely entail a discussion of the institution's priorities and goals and related success metrics surrounding persistence, retention, and graduation. The importance of having sound, verifiable data cannot be overemphasized.

Creating an initial first-year seminar or revising an existing course is a huge undertaking that will require the participation and collaboration of colleagues from across the campus. It will, no doubt, impact a number of long-standing processes and procedures. Colleges are steeped in traditions that have, until recently, withstood the test of time. The realities of life in the 21st century and pressure from outside groups are forcing colleges to reexamine practices that have been in place for decades. This will necessitate a shift in thinking that will likely be uncomfortable for some stakeholders.

Most resistance to change initiatives is rooted in the prevailing culture of an organization. When long-standing practices are challenged, it can be common for individuals who helped to create or uphold these practices to become defensive. Despite evidence that the practices are no longer effective or need change, the stakeholders may perceive the changes as a criticism of their work. Helping members of the organization understand that change is not personal but necessary for the greater good requires looking at the deeper nature of the issue. This often means discussing "undiscussable" topics such as low success rates. People only discuss "undiscussable" or uncomfortable topics when they possess the reflection and inquiry skills needed to honestly talk about multifaceted, conflict-laden issues without provoking defensiveness (Senge, 1999, p. 9). Using data to provide the context for these types of discussions can soften individuals' defensive barriers, resulting in meaningful and productive conversations.

Too often, faculty and staff make decisions based on anecdotal experiences rather than data. In many instances, professionals may have a skewed view of student issues and performance because of whom they interact with daily. For example, a professional staff member who is working almost exclusively with honor students would likely have a very different perspective on student experiences and outcomes as compared to a professional staff member who is working almost exclusively with students on probation. In both situations, it is critical to shift the focus from the small subset of students to the overall student body. Policies and practices should not be developed based on a few isolated instances but rather on a comprehensive understanding of the issues and related success metrics for the entire student population.

There are several ways to combat the extensive focus on special circumstances or exceptions to the rule. First, directing attention toward the student body can help. This can be done by asking questions such as these:

- What percentage of the student population is facing this issue?
- What data exist to suggest that this is an issue for many students?

Focusing the conversation on data that represents a significant portion of the student body is important.

Another approach that is helpful when faced with a faculty or staff member who frequently brings up issues that may sidetrack the conversation is to encourage everyone involved to view the situation from another lens. For example, asking faculty and staff to view the issue from the perspective of another professional on campus, or even more importantly from the student perspective, can help highlight the need for change. After reviewing the success metrics, most, if not all, will agree that we can and need to do better for our students. It is important to respectfully address faculty and staff who focus on specific situations that are not typical of most students.

Questioning can be a powerful technique to raise awareness and determine what institutional interventions need to change.

> The injunction against discovering and asking questions is wide-spread in today's family, educational, and corporate cultures. That's unfortunate, because asking questions that matter is one of the primary ways that people have, starting in childhood, to engage their natural, self-organizing capacities for collaborative conversation, exploration inquiry, and learning. Asking questions is essential for coevolving the "futures we want" rather than being forced to live with the "futures we get." (Senge, 1999, p. 507)

To effectively use questioning to facilitate change, the first-year seminar course coordinator and his or her team can ask the following questions at a meeting with key stakeholders:

- What are the current retention rates at our institution?
- What are the current transfer and/or graduation rates at our institution?
- Are we satisfied with these current success rates?
- Based on national and institutional data, what factors contribute the most to successful outcomes? For example, has your institution used the National Survey of Student Engagement or Community College Survey of Student Engagement or other national benchmark data? (Center for Community College Student Engagement, 2014; Center for Post-Secondary Research, 2018)
- What are the institutional priorities?
- What does the strategic plan say about student success?

- What does the data say about the effectiveness of the first-year seminar? Here, you can refer back to chapter 2 and also the infographic in appendix A.
- How can the first-year seminar help students achieve program and institutional goals?

Faculty and staff are more likely to respond positively to data that are effectively packaged in visual charts and graphs. Graphs that illustrate academic performance or graduation rates can tell the important story about student success and direct audience attention to the key issues. Research shows that we can understand and remember content when visual images, charts, or graphs are used (Mayer, 2009). For examples of how to effectively use visuals to communicate data, refer to the infographics in appendix A.

In addition to using images as appropriate, it can also be very helpful to draw attention to key data points or research findings. Rather than sharing endless numbers of studies with others on campus, identify the key studies and any related institutional-specific data. Focus faculty and staff attention on these studies. This approach prevents information overload and increases understanding and retention of the material. However, have additional data available should faculty or staff want to see more information.

There will be members of the campus community who have had little reason to use or interest in using data to make their case. Some members of the campus community may feel threatened by the data. When presenting data to colleagues, their reluctance should be acknowledged, but they should be engaged in conversations that show how the data can be used as a catalyst for change. Even when the data clearly make the case for change, it is important to remember that a deeply ingrained culture, multiple layers of bureaucracy, low levels of trust, lack of teamwork, and the all-too-human fear of the unknown are hurdles that all institutions must address when embarking on a large-scale change initiative (Kotter, 1996).

Mindset and what faculty, staff, administrators, and students think of the course is another challenge associated with making the case for the first-year seminar. Although you may have engaged in a significant redesign process, many may still view the course as it was previously taught. If the first-year seminar was not perceived in a positive light, it can take time to shift this mindset. The key here is to emphasize how the course learning outcomes and assignments have shifted, demonstrating the value of the course for all students.

Not surprisingly, first-year seminars with a stronger academic versus extended orientation focus are more likely to be well-received by faculty. Thus, it can be helpful to emphasize and highlight the academic components of the course. In addition, drawing attention to how the newly revised curriculum aligns to Guided Pathways can also be helpful.

Sometimes changing the name of the course is a good strategy, especially in situations where many faculty and staff have negative perceptions of the previous iteration of the course. In addition to a new course name, revising the course description may also be needed. Clearly communicating the goals and purpose of the first-year seminar as part of a student's overall educational experience is important.

Identifying and Training Faculty

Staffing of first-year seminars can vary within institutions as well as across institutions. For example, instructors may be student affairs professionals, full-time academic faculty, adjunct faculty, or graduate students. Karp et al. (2012) argue that colleges should make instructional choices that foster a learning-for-application classroom environment. Questions about the credentials needed to teach the first-year seminar frequently appear on the listserv sponsored by the National Resource Center on the First-Year Experience and Students in Transition.

Coordinators of the course struggle with defining the qualifications for teaching the course. Although having a strong background in student development and career exploration can be quite helpful, Cuseo (n.d.b.) suggests that the discipline expertise may be less important than other characteristics such as a "student-centered educational philosophy," "use of engaging pedagogy," "genuine interest in advising and mentoring new students," and "evidence of commitment to out-of-class contact with students" (para. 2), to name a few. Groccia and Hunter (2012) note that the best first-year instructors are those who not only enjoy the content of the course but also find it rewarding to teach first-year college students. Whatever staffing decisions are made, instructors need to be comfortable with interactive, reflective, and guided practice pedagogies (Karp et al., 2012).

According to results of the 2012–2013 National Survey of First-Year Seminars, first-year seminars were mostly taught by tenure-track faculty, but non-tenured faculty, student affairs professionals, adjuncts, and graduate assistants were often teaching the course (Young & Hopp, 2014). Not surprisingly, results of this survey revealed that adjuncts were more likely to teach the first-year seminar course at community colleges while it was more common for tenure-track faculty to teach the course at four-year colleges.

The nature of the instructors also varied by the type of course. For example, student affairs professionals were more likely to teach first-year seminars with an extended orientation approach while tenure-track faculty were more likely to teach first-year seminars with an academic-uniform or academic-variable approach. First-year seminars with a study skill approach were most likely to be taught by adjunct faculty (Young & Hopp, 2014).

The use of dedicated first-year seminar instructors can lend value and legitimacy to the course and help raise its profile across the campus, provided that they are skilled teachers with time to acquire the specialized course knowledge and hone their pedagogical skills to effectively promote learning-for-application within the classroom. A benefit of hiring full-time first-year seminar instructors is that there is an increased likelihood of expertise in the discipline. Most full-time faculty hired specifically to teach the first-year seminar have a strong background in student development, education, psychology, or a related field.

Many colleges and universities utilize full-time faculty from across different disciplines. One of the advantages of this approach is that faculty are aware of the academic challenges of entering students. Another advantage is that tenure-track faculty members are available to students during office hours and often have an in-depth knowledge of the campus culture and resources that can be very helpful to first-year students.

Having faculty from a variety of disciplines is especially important if colleges or universities are using discipline-specific or meta-majors approaches to the first-year seminar. The challenge, of course, with this approach is that most faculty members from disciplines outside of the first-year experience probably do not have expertise in the first-year seminar curriculum.

In other words, faculty from different disciplines such as the sciences or business may not have strong content knowledge in career exploration or study skills, two primary areas of focus in the course. Over the years, many student success professionals have noticed that when faculty do not feel comfortable with the first-year seminar curriculum, the course becomes heavily focused on the discipline, sometimes becoming an introduction to the introductory course in the discipline. When this happens, the integrity and the effectiveness of the course are jeopardized. Training faculty in the first-year seminar curriculum can obviously help address these concerns and help ensure that the curriculum is being implemented effectively.

Professional development that targets the course content is therefore critical. While this training will be especially helpful for faculty members in outside departments, even instructors with a background related to the first-year seminar will find training valuable. First-year seminar instructors may have a strong background knowledge in some of the course content, but not have expertise in all the first-year seminar curriculum. For example, instructors may have a strong background in building academic skills, but their knowledge of the career exploration process may be minimal. Another example could be a new instructor who may know the content well but may not be familiar with the campus resources.

More specifically, training for first-year seminar instructors should address all the course content areas. To return to the New Jersey community college example, this would mean that training would need to address the following areas:

- Career exploration and academic planning
- Purpose and structure of higher education
- Goal setting
- Decision making, critical thinking, and information literacy
- Grit and resilience
- Self-reflection
- Study strategies
- Financial literacy

Although the first-year seminar coordinator is often the one who organizes and often provides the training for instructors, it can be helpful to also utilize the expertise of colleagues from across campus. For example, counseling and advising professionals can provide training on career exploration and academic planning; education and psychology faculty can provide training on topics such as goal setting, grit and resilience, and study strategies; librarians can provide training on information literacy; and business faculty or financial aid professionals can provide training on financial literacy.

Professional development targeting general teaching skills is important for all faculty but is especially important for first-year seminar instructors. As Groccia and Hunter (2012) note, most faculty have been hired because of their content expertise not because of their pedagogical expertise. In other words, we can assume that faculty members teaching chemistry have expertise in chemistry and faculty members teaching psychology have expertise in psychology. Despite expertise in their discipline, it is very possible and perhaps even probable that these faculty members have little to no training in how to teach. Although some graduate programs are now adding teaching courses to the curriculum, many of the faculty across the nation have never taken a single course on teaching and learning.

Fortunately, most colleges and universities have established teaching and learning centers that provide faculty development focused on effective pedagogical practices. "Research has shown that investment in faculty development leads to positive student outcomes" (Haras, Taylor, Sorcinelli, & van Hoene, 2017, p. 13). In addition to college- or university-wide teaching and learning support, department- and course-level training can be provided. Most colleges and universities offer professional development specifically related to the first-year seminar (Groccia & Hunter, 2012). First-year seminar instructors will benefit from the same type of professional development as their peers teaching in other disciplines. Student engagement, while important in all courses, is especially critical in the first-year seminar course given the learning goals of the course.

Training is particularly important for first-year seminar instructors because students who have positive academic experiences during their first semester are much more likely to continue in college and achieve their goals. For example, students who develop a strong sense of belonging are more likely to have higher levels of academic self-efficacy (Freeman, Anderson, & Jensen, 2007), which is typically associated with higher levels of achievement. Instructors will benefit from professional development aimed at assisting students with making connections while also increasing academic skills. More specifically, the following teaching and learning topics would be helpful to focus on during instructor training:

- Engaging and motivating students
- Utilizing active learning and group work approaches
- Facilitating meaningful discussions
- Effective use of technology
- Giving effective feedback to facilitate learning

In-person trainings are advantageous because the facilitator or speaker can model best practices and engage instructors in activities that can be used in class. Instructors appreciate having face-to-face time to celebrate success stories and problem-solve challenging situations. However, finding a day and time that works for all instructors can be quite a challenging task, sometimes even an impossible one. Thus, online training options should also be considered. In-person trainings can be recorded or better yet, separate online videos can be created to serve as resources to new instructors as well as for current instructors to refer back to and use as needed.

In addition to traditional workshops that can be offered in person or online, it can be advantageous to engage first-year seminar instructors in other professional development opportunities. For example, giving first-year instructors an opportunity to observe fellow instructors' courses and the sharing of practices and materials with each other can be incredibly helpful (Karp et al., 2012). At many colleges and universities, regular meetings are held for instructors throughout the year with programming and conversations targeting discipline-specific content and best pedagogical practices. This ongoing approach to professional development is ideal.

Creating Campus Excitement

With data in hand and a plan for moving forward, garnering support for a mandatory three-credit first-year experience course will require recruiting a team of like-minded individuals. According to Kotter (1996), major transformational change is not accomplished by one individual. It requires developing the right vision, communicating it to large numbers of people, eliminating major obstacles, generating short-term wins, leading and managing a multitude of change projects, and firmly establishing these new approaches within the organizational culture.

> A strong guiding coalition is always needed—one with the right composition, level of trust, and shared objective. Building such a team is always an essential part of the early stages of any effort to restructure, reengineer, or retool a set of strategies. (Kotter, 1996, p. 52)

The first step in creating major change is to establish a sense of urgency. This can be done by presenting data that make a compelling argument for change. It will be important to establish and maintain a strong working relationship with the campus's institutional research office in order to generate data on such measures as retention rates, persistence rates, and graduation rates. These data will need to be benchmarked against national data in order to situate the institution within the larger, national conversation on student success.

It is important to note, however, that it is not always necessary to gather institutional-specific data. In many cases, the national data are quite compelling and replicating the national findings at the local level may not be the best use of institutional time and resources. The need for institutional-level data is one that is often best determined by the campus culture. Once the stage is set, creating a guiding coalition with enough power to lead the change effort is the next (second) step in the process (Kotter, 1996).

In selecting the members of the guiding coalition, it is important to include a cross-section of the campus community. Key members of the team should include full-time faculty with experience teaching the course. At many institutions, part-time faculty comprise the majority of individuals teaching first-year seminar courses Many of them are seasoned teachers with years of experience teaching the course. If this is the case, they should also be part of the guiding coalition.

If the course is housed in an academic department, the department chairperson or course coordinator should also be included. Having members that have strong pedagogical backgrounds, administrative expertise, and an understanding of the principles and value of the first-year seminar will be critical in addressing the questions that will arise as the initiative to establish the first-year seminar as a required, credit-bearing course moves forward.

Student services professionals, such as counselors, advisors, librarians, orientation specialists, career services managers, experiential learning coordinators, and other such course advocates should also be part of the coalition. Most seminar courses work closely with a variety of student services offices to introduce students to the various resources available to them. Individuals who work directly with seminar students outside of the classroom, or in conjunction with the instructors, bring a perspective that provides a more complete picture of the breadth and depth of the course. In the end, the coalition should be comprised of members who are in positions of power, possess expertise in a variety of areas, have good reputations, and have proven leadership skills (Kotter, 1996).

Once the guiding coalition is in place, the third step in the process is to create a vision to direct the change effort and strategies for achieving the vision (Kotter, 1996). Building on the data that establish the sense of urgency, the vision should remain simple and straightforward. The overarching vision is to increase the success of students so that they achieve their education and career goals. One of the strategies for realizing that vision is the establishment of a three-credit, first-year seminar course for all students. Aligning the course with the principles of the Guided Pathways movement provides the framework for implementing the strategy.

The fourth step in the process is communicating the vision to the larger campus community. Advocating for large-scale change requires a widespread communication plan to ensure that all members of the campus community have been informed and given the opportunity to provide feedback. The communication plan should be simple, focused, and jargon-free, suitable for all audiences, whether they are students, faculty, staff, board of trustees, or the general public (Kotter, 1996). Key messages should be developed to target specific audiences. The messages should answer three questions: "Why? Why now? Why will we succeed?" (Achieving the Dream, n.d., p. 45).

To ensure that the messages reach their intended audiences, they should be delivered using a variety of media such as email, social media, websites, meetings, memos, and print materials. There should also be opportunity for feedback. Two-way discussions are needed to help people answer all of the questions that arise during a significant change effort (Kotter, 1996). If the plan is to be effectively communicated, members of the coalition must not only be good communicators, they must also possess good listening skills.

The guiding coalition members are the facilitators of change. Large-scale change occurs only through the efforts of many individuals. Student success initiatives like Guided Pathways in general, and first-year seminar reform specifically, require the involvement of many individuals. To effect large-scale change (step five in the process), these individuals must feel empowered to act. This entails identifying and removing as many barriers or issues that are preventing the change from taking place. These barriers are often associated with structures, skills, systems, and supervisors (Kotter, 1996). To move the initiative forward, the guiding coalition should identify and address as many barriers as possible.

For instance, the members should look at the structure of the college's programs to identify how the first-year seminar course can fit within the degree requirements. If there is no place in the curriculum for the seminar, this may prompt a discussion about revising the course to meet general education requirements or advocating for the course to be a campus-wide graduation requirement.

The skills of the first-year seminar instructors are also an important consideration. Offering the course to all students in the institution may result in a shortage of qualified instructors. Ample training and professional development opportunities must be in place to ensure that new instructors are skilled in the pedagogy of first-year seminars and are qualified to teach the course. At the same time, on-going training and development for experienced instructors must not be ignored. Seasoned instructors should be kept apprised of developments in the field so that they maintain currency in the classroom.

From a systems perspective, it bears reiterating that the first-year seminar is one aspect of a comprehensive student success initiative. As such, guiding coalition members need to consider the role of the course within that context. Most institutions have broad-based systems in place that acclimate and engage entering students. These systems usually involve the services of a variety of offices such as testing, admissions, registrar, advising, financial aid, and counseling. There are often high levels of coordination between these areas to ensure that the on-boarding process for new students is comprehensive and effective.

For some colleges, the on-boarding process ends when students begin their first semester of classes. For other schools, on-boarding continues through the first semester, while at other institutions it continues through the first academic year. Members need to understand the larger picture in order to effectively advocate for a mandatory first-year seminar. Highlighting how the first-year seminar can be used to assist students with exploring career options, developing essential success skills, and engaging in academic and career planning and decision making can demonstrate the value of the course within the Guided Pathways context.

Barriers associated with institutional culture are difficult to eliminate entirely. However, smaller barriers within systems can be addressed. In some cases, there may be an administrator or critical faculty member who may not see the value of the first-year seminar and therefore does not want to see the course be required of all students. All organizations have people who, for a variety of reasons, are resistant to change. Because initiating transformative change involves many individuals, it is likely that a guiding coalition will face this challenge. It can occur at any level, from a faculty member, director, or dean, to a member of executive leadership.

Unfortunately, there is no easy solution. Rather than attempting to work around the individual, honest dialogue is often the best approach. Ideally, one or more members of the coalition will need to have an in-depth conversation about the initiative. It is always helpful to view the situation from several different viewpoints; a good first step is listening to concerns about mandating the first-year seminar course. Once there is a good understanding of the concerns, the conversation can shift toward the common goal of student success. Then, determine the best way to proceed, ask for their cooperation, and offer whatever assistance is needed to support student success (Kotter, 1996). This is not an enviable task, but one that is sometimes necessary to keep the momentum moving forward.

Generating short-term wins is the sixth step in the change process. Because large-scale change takes time, the importance of short-term wins cannot be ignored. Not only do they boost morale and motivation, they also justify short-term costs, help refine vision and strategy, silence the critics, and keep key players engaged. A good short-term win has at least three characteristics: it is visible, unambiguous, and directly related to the change initiative (Kotter, 1996). For a first-year seminar course, an example of a short-term win might be having the course approved as a graduation requirement or replacing a non-credit seminar with a three-credit seminar. No matter what, it is important to make sure that short-term wins are recognized, publicized, and celebrated.

Consolidating gains and producing more change is the seventh step in the process and closely related to step six. It is important to acknowledge short-term gains, but not at the expense of the long-term vision. "Whenever you let up before the job is done, critical momentum can be lost and regression may follow" (Kotter, 1996, p. 133).

Once regression starts, regaining momentum can be a herculean undertaking. Only the most stalwart of campus champions will continue the process (Kotter, 1996). Therefore, it is important to build on the credibility of short-term wins and continue to work on the larger aspects of the change initiative. For instance, if the non-credit first-year seminar course is approved as a three-credit course but is still not required of all students, that short-term win should be used as leverage to mandate the course for all students. Guiding coalitions must always keep their eye on the long-term vision for change.

The eighth and final step in the transformative change process is anchoring the new approaches in the culture (Kotter, 1996). The power of culture in higher education cannot be underestimated. As Mehaffy (2010) observed,

> We confront rapid changes in the circumstances and context in which public higher education operates and yet we seem unable to respond with the creative and innovative solutions that will ensure our success. Someone recently said that the core problem is that higher education was designed in the 11th century and operates on a 19th century agrarian calendar, while trying to prepare students for life and work in the 21st century. (p. 2)

"Culture changes only after you have successfully altered people's actions, after the new behavior produces some group benefit for a period of time, and after people see the connection between the new actions and the performance improvement" (Kotter, 1996, p. 158). Once a mandatory three-credit first-year seminar course is established, the work of the guiding coalition is not done. To ensure that the course becomes a lasting and integrated part of the institution's culture, the members must diligently track course outcomes, share the results with the campus community, openly receive feedback, and make course refinements when needed.

A continual loop of inquiry and reflection will help to ensure that the course contributes to the larger goal of improving the long-term success of all students. The first-year seminar can be an incredibly important foundational component of Guided Pathways, but for colleges and universities to fully engage in Guided Pathways work, the first-year seminar can only be viewed as part of the solution, not the entire solution. Additional supports must be put into place to support students throughout their educational journey.

In summary, requiring the first-year seminar course of all students can reduce equity gaps and increase student success outcomes. Ideally, the first-year seminar should be included in all programs as a general education or other requirement. Another option, which is not as ideal, is to require the course as a graduation requirement.

To make the case for the first-year seminar, data on current success metrics as well as on the impact of the first-year seminar are needed. A guiding coalition of advocates for the course can then work to garner support for institutional changes aimed at providing all students with meaningful opportunities for career exploration and success skill development. If the guiding coalition is successful and a three-credit first-year seminar course is required of all students, then the real winners are the students who will be more likely to meet with success.

REFERENCES

Achieving the Dream (n.d.). *Integrated student support redesign Toolkit: A toolkit for redesigning advising and student services to effectively support every student.* Retrieved from http://achievingthedream.org/resource/17257/integrated-student-support-redesign-toolkit

Bailey, T. R., Jaggars, S. S., & Jenkins, D. (2015). *Redesigning America's community colleges.* Cambridge, MA: Harvard University Press.

Barry, N. M., & Dannenberg, M. (April 2016). *The high cost of inadequate high schools and high school student achievement on college affordability.* (ERN Policy Brief). Washington, DC: Education Reform Now. Retrieved from https://edreformnow.org/wp-content/uploads/2016/04/EdReformNow-O-O-P-Embargoed-Final.pdf

Bensimon, E. (Fall 2005). Closing the achievement gap in higher education: An organizational learning perspective. *New Directions for Higher Education, 131,* 99–111.

Blanton, K., McLaughlin, J., & Niese, M. (n.d.). *FYE continuous quality improvement.* Unpublished document.

Center for Community College Student Engagement (2014). *A matter of degrees: Practices to pathways.* Retrieved from https://postsecondary.gatesfoundation.org/wp-content/uploads/2014/09/CCSSE-Report_Matter_of_Degrees_3.pdf

Center for Post-Secondary Research (2018). *National survey of student engagement.* Indiana University of Education. Retrieved from http://nsse.indiana.edu/

Center for Community College Student Engagement (2018). *Community college survey of student engagement.* The University of Texas at Austin. Retrieved from http://www.ccsse.org/

Couturier, L. K. and Cullinane, J. (May 2015). *A call to action to improve math placement policies and processes.* Jobs for the Future, http://www.jff.org/publications/call-action-improve-math-placement-policies-and-processes

Cuseo, J. (n.d.a.). *The empirical case for the first-year seminar: Evidence of course impact on student retention, persistence to graduation, and academic achievement.* Unpublished manuscript.

Cuseo, J. (n.d.b.) *Recruitment and selection of faculty as first-year seminar instructors.* Unpublished manuscript.

Du, F. (2016). Using National Survey of Student Engagement (NSSE) findings to enhance the cocurricular and advising aspects of a first-year seminar. *Assessment Update: Progress, Trends, and Practices in Higher Education, 28*(3), 1–2.

Freeman, T. M., Anderson, L. H., & Jensen, J. M. (2007). Sense of belonging in college freshmen at the class-room and campus levels. *The Journal of Experimental Education, 75*, 203–220, https://doi.org/10.3200/JEXE.75.3.203-220

Groccia, J. E., & Hunter, M. S. (2012). *The first-year seminar: Designing, implementing, and assessing courses to support student learning and success: Vol. II. Instructor training and development.* Columbia, SC: University of South Carolina, National Resource Center for the First-Year Experience and Students in Transition.

Haras, D., Taylor, S. C., Sorcinelli, M. D., & von Hoene, L. (2017). Institutional commitment to teaching excellence: Assessing the impacts and outcomes of faculty development. Washington, DC: American Council on Education.

Jenkins, D. (2014). *Redesigning community colleges for student success: Overview of the Guided Pathways approach.* Community College Research Center, Teachers College, Columbia University.

Jessup-Anger, J. E. (2011). What's the point? An exploration of students' motivation to learn in a first-year seminar. *The Journal of General Education, 60*(2), 101–116.

Karp, M. M., Bickerstaff, S., Rucks-Ahidiana, Z., Bork, R. H., Barragan, M., & Edgecombe, N. (2012). *College 101 courses for applied learning and student success.* (CCRC Working Paper No. 49). New York, NY: Columbia University, Teachers College, Community College Research Center.

Karp, M. M, Raufman, J., Efthimiou, C., & Ritze, N. (2015). *Redesigning a student success course for sustained impact: Early outcomes findings.* (CCRC Working Paper No. 81). New York, NY: Columbia University, Teachers College, Community College Research Center.

Kotter, J. P. (1996). *Leading change.* Boston, MA: Harvard Business School Press.

Mayer, R. E. (2009). *Multimedia learning* (2nd ed.). New York: Cambridge University Press.

Mehaffy, G. L. (2010). The red balloon project; Re-imagining undergraduate education. Retrieved from http://www.jsu.edu/redballoon/docs/Red_Balloon_Project_Description_June_2010_1_.pdf

Permzadian, V., & Crede, M. (2016). Do first-year seminars improve college grades and retention? A quantitative review of their overall effectiveness and an examination of moderators of effectiveness. *Review of Educational Research, 86*(1) 277–316.

Senge, P. (1999). *The dance of change.* New York, NY: Doubleday.

Vandal, B. (June 23, 2015). *The results are in. Corequisite remediation works.* Indianapolis, IN: Complete College America. Retrieved from https://completecollege.org/article/the-results-are-in-corequisite-remediation-works/

Young, D. G., & Hopp, J. M. (2014). *2012–2013 National Survey of First-Year Seminars: Exploring high-impact practices in the first college year.* (Research Report No. 4). Columbia, SC: University of South Carolina, National Resource Center for The First-Year Experience and Students in Transition.

Appendix A

Making the Case Infographic

The First-Year Seminar: Retention and Persistence

Students who take the first-year seminar course, as opposed to those who don't, are more likely to continue in college.

(Ben-Avie et al., 2012; Boudreau & Kromney, 1994; Bushko, 1995; Cho & Karp, 2013; Dahlgren, 2008; Derby & Smith, 2004; Fralick, 2008; Griffin & Romm, 2008; Jackson, 2005)

Students who took the first-year seminar at Widener University were 18% more likely to attend college as sophomores

Bushko (1995)

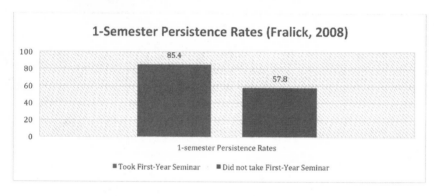

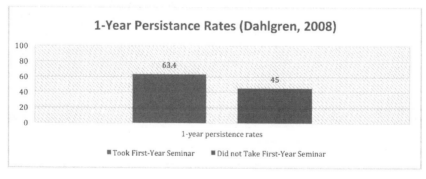

The First-Year Seminar: Academic Performance

Students who take the first-year seminar course, as opposed to those who don't, are more likely to perform well academically.

(Ben-Avie et al., 2012; Boudreau & Kromney, 1994; Dahlgren, 2008; House, 2005; Jenkins-Guarnier et al., 2015; Jajairam, 2016; Jamelske, 2008; Karp et al., 2015; Schwartz & Grieve, 2008)

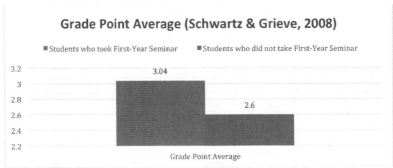

Grade Point Average (Schwartz & Grieve, 2008)

■ Students who took First-Year Seminar   ■ Students who did not take First-Year Seminar

Note: Students had similar academic performance at the start of the semester as measured by high school grades and ACT scores.

Academic Benefits of First-Year Seminar can be Long-Lasting

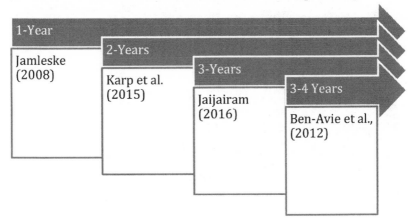

The First-Year Seminar: Graduation Rates

Students who take the first-year seminar course, as opposed to those who don't, are more likely to graduate.

(Blowers & Elling, 2005; Pascarella & Terenzini, 2005; Schnell, Louis, & Doetkott, 2003; Smith & Derby, 2004; Zeidenberg, Jenkins, & Calcagno, 2007)

Students who took the first-year seminar were 8% more likely than their peers to earn a credential

Zeidenberg, Jenkins, & Calcagno (2007)

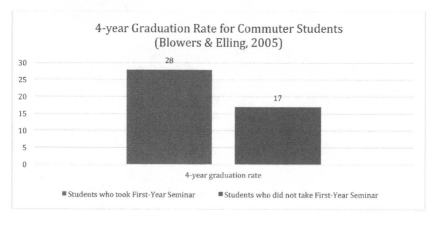

4-year Graduation Rate for Commuter Students
(Blowers & Elling, 2005)

■ Students who took First-Year Seminar   ■ Students who did not take First-Year Seminar

Based on a review of over 40 studies, researchers have found that students who take the first-year seminar are more likely to graduate within four years as compared to peers who did not take the course (Pascarella & Terenzini, 2005).

The First-Year Seminar: Career Decision Making

Students who take the first-year seminar course, as opposed to those who don't, are more likely to make better informed career decisions.

(Adams, Thomas, & McDaniel, 2008; Blowers & Elling, 2005; Fox & Esler, 2005; Jaijaram, 2016; Peterson & Stubblefield, 2008)

 85% of students who took a first-year seminar course reported having a better sense of career options.
(Jaijaram, 2016)

Students who took the first-year seminar reported increased knowledge of career choices and resources.
(Peterson & Stubblefield, 2008)

Survey Questions	Before the First-Year Seminar	After the First-Year Seminar
I know what careers might interest me.	2.15	3.1
I am familiar with tools and resources for exploring majors and careers.	1.8	3.1

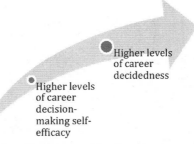

Higher levels of career decidedness

Higher levels of career decision-making self-efficacy

Students who took a first-year seminar course had higher levels of career decision making self-efficacy and decidedness, as compared to students who did not take the course.
(Adams, Thomas, & McDaniel, 2008)

The First-Year Seminar:
Does it Benefit All Students?

Students of all ability levels, not just those who are considered at-risk,
benefit from taking the first-year seminar course.

(Howard & Jones, 2000; Miller, Janz, & Chen, 2007; Permzadian & Crede, 2016; Pittendrigh et al., 2016)

Students of all abilities who took the first-year seminar course were
more likely to continue in college than their peers
who did not take the course.

(Miller, Janz, & Chen, 2007)

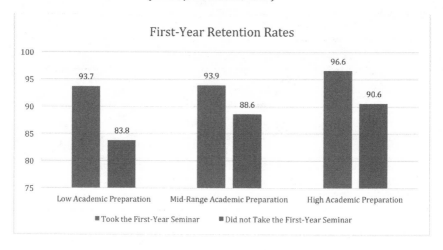

First-Year Retention Rates

 Most effective: Required of all
incoming students.

Least effective: Required only of
academically underprepared students.

Based on a meta-analytic review of first-year seminars, efficacy was
highest in courses where all incoming students were required to take
the course (Permzadian & Crede, 2016).

Appendix B

Sample Syllabus

Welcome to First-Year Seminar!

Insert Course Code

Insert Meeting Dates and Times

Insert Professor Contact Information:

Professor Name
Email Address
Office Location
Office Hours

What is this course all about?

Please come and visit me!

Customize this welcome section (consider adding your photo)

Welcome to the course! I am excited to be your instructor and can't wait to get to know you. Throughout the semester, we will be talking about your goals and career plans and strategies that will help you be successful. I hope that you will view me as part of your support team. In addition to teaching you research-based success strategies, I am here to help you plan for success, problem-solve as needed, and celebrate successful experiences. My official office hours are listed above, but I'm more than happy to find a different day and time to meet if these do not work well for your schedule. I believe that it's really important for us to talk outside of class so please connect with me before or after class, stop by my office (or make an appointment), and e-mail me!

What book and other materials do I need?

Text: *Student Success in College: Doing What Works! 3ʳᵈ edition, Cengage*

What is this course all about?

Course Description:

This course is designed to help you explore career options, set meaningful academic and career goals, develop essential skills such as information literacy and critical thinking skills, and engage in academic behaviors and study strategies that will help you meet with success.

Learning Outcomes: What will be able to do after successfully completing this course?

You will develop a higher sense of self-efficacy by:

1. Identifying and utilizing strategies and resources that promote academic success, personal growth, and resilience.
2. Demonstrating critical thinking, information literacy, and technological skills.
3. Practicing interpersonal and leadership skills essential in a diverse, global society.
4. Reflecting on values, goals, decisions, and actions in relation to their impact on self and others.
5. Creating academic, career and financial plans.

Course Content Areas: What topics will we discuss?

- Purpose, value, and structure of higher education
- Goal setting, career exploration, and choosing a career path
- Decision making, critical thinking and information literacy
- Academic/Study strategies including how to read and use scholarly research
- Soft skills such as time and project management, interpersonal skills and leadership
- Academic, career, and financial planning
- Grit, resilience, and motivation
- Self-reflection and monitoring progress

What can I expect to happen during class?

Being actively involved and engaged with the course content will result in higher levels of learning and skill development. The semester will therefore be filled with lively discussions, activities, and challenging assignments. Because we learn best when engaged with others, you will work with a partner or small group almost every time we meet.

Important Policy Information (Customize)

If you need accommodations due to a disability, please reach out to a Disability Service Provider.

To foster a productive learning environment, the College requires that all students adhere to the Code of Student Conduct which is published in the college catalog and on the college's website.

Academic Integrity Policy:
All Students are Expected to Engage in Academically Honest Work

Academic integrity benefits everyone in our community. It not only helps you reach the real goal of this class- learning, but also allows for the college and program to be perceived positively by others. When students are dishonest, they lose out on valuable learning that will help them perform well in their career. It can also negatively impact all of the students in the program and at the institution by creating negative mindsets which may result in fewer outside learning opportunities for students. Academic dishonesty is any attempt by a student to gain academic advantage through dishonest means or to assist another student with gaining an unfair advantage. Academic integrity is important regardless of whether the work is graded or ungraded, group or individual, written or oral. Dishonest acts can result in a failing grade on an assignment, a failing course grade and/or an official code of conduct charge being filed.

Late/Missed Work Policy:
All Students are Expected to Complete Learning Tasks on Schedule

It is important to stay on track with your assignments- not only will this help you feel less stressed but it is also an important skill you will need in your career. Being able to meet deadlines and juggle many tasks is an important career and life skill. Thus, it is expected that you will complete all assignments according to the schedule. This is particularly important when working as a part of a team as others will be counting on you. If you have a personal situation that prevents you from doing so, please discuss this with me prior to the due date so we can explore options. Assignments can be submitted via MindTap **PRIOR to a class** if you will be absent.

Registrar Withdrawal Information

Students sometimes have a need to withdraw from a class due to personal or academic reasons. *Click here for deadline dates.* If you do encounter difficulties, please contact me prior to withdrawing.

Available Help and Support: (Customize)

Successful people access support from others as needed. The college has many support services that can help you achieve your goals. I encourage you to reach out to me or other professionals on campus as needed. Here's some information about the resources available to you:

Your Professor	Add email and/or phone contact information
Librarians	Add library website
Tutors	Add tutoring website
Advisors	Add advising website
Counseling Services (including Disability Services)	Add counseling website

Your Learning Experience: What do you have to do in this course?

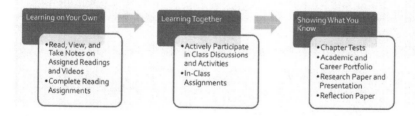

Traditional Course Outline

Class Date	What is Due?	Topic, Activities, and Relevant Resources
Week 1	Reading Assignment: Getting Started and Chapter 1	Welcome and Introductions Introduction: Getting Started Chapter 1: Discovering the Value of Education and Sharpening Key Thinking Skills
Week 2	Reading Assignment: Chapter 2 Read Research Articles: Howard & Jones (2000); Travis (2011)	Chapter 1: Discovering the Value of Education and Sharpening Key Thinking Skills Chapter 2: Setting Goals and Choosing a Career Path
Week 3	Academic and Career Portfolio: Complete Self-Assessment Assignments Chapter 1 Test	Chapter 2: Setting Goals and Choosing a Career Path
Week 4	Reading Assignment: Chapter 3 Chapter 2 Test	Chapter 3: Building Academic Skills Library Visit
Week 5	Academic and Career Portfolio: Career Information and Presentation	Chapter 3: Building Academic Skills Career Presentations
Week 6	Reading Assignment: Chapter 4 Read Research Article: Deepa & Seth (2013) Chapter 3 Test	Chapter 4: Strengthening Soft Skills
Week 7	Reading Assignment: Chapter 5 Academic and Career Portfolio: Educational and Financial Plan Assignment Chapter 4 Test	Chapter 5: Demonstrating Knowledge and Skills Advising/Registration Prep Session
Week 8	Bring 4 research articles to class Read Research Article: Oliver & Kowalczyk (2013)	GROUP WORK: Reviewing Articles and Selecting Article for Presentation Chapter 5: Demonstrating Knowledge and Skills
Week 9	Reading Assignment: Chapter 6 Chapter 5 Test	Chapter 6: Mapping Your Path to Success: Plans and Action Steps
Week 10	Exploring the Research in Summary Worksheet Due	GROUP WORK: Focus on understanding research article Demonstrating Knowledge and Skills Chapter 6: Mapping Your Path to Success: Plans and Action Steps
Week 11	Reading Assignment: Chapter 7 Power Point Slides Due Chapter 6 Test	Chapter 7: Staying on Track and Celebrating Success
Week 12	Academic and Career Portfolio: Career Networking Actions and Reflection Assignment	GROUP WORK: Creating a master presentation slides and focus on delivery
Week 13	Research Presentations	Presentations on Student Success Research
Week 14	Reflection Paper Due Chapter 7 Test	Chapter 7: Staying on Track and Celebrating Success

Backwards Design Course Outline

Class Date	What is Due?	Topic, Activities, and Relevant Resources
Week 1	Reading Assignment: Getting Started and Chapter 1	Welcome and Introductions Introduction: Getting Started Chapter 1: Discovering the Value of Education and Sharpening Key Thinking Skills
Week 2	Reading Assignment: Chapter 2	Chapter 2: Setting Goals and Choosing a Career Path
Week 3	Academic and Career Portfolio: Complete Self-Assessment Assignments Reading Assignment: Chapter 4	Chapter 4: Strengthening Soft Skills
Week 4	Academic and Career Portfolio: Career Information and Presentation Reading Assignment: Chapter 6 Chapter Tests: Chapter 2	Chapter 6: Mapping Your Path to Success: Plans and Action Steps Career Presentations
Week 5	Academic and Career Portfolio: Career Networking Actions and Reflection Assignment Reading Assignment: Chapter 5	Chapter 5: Demonstrating Knowledge and Skills
Week 6	Academic and Career Portfolio: Educational and Financial Plan Assignment Chapter Tests: Chapter 5 and 6	Advising/Registration Prep Session
Week 7	**Final Academic and Career Portfolio Due**	Chapter 1: Discovering the Value of Education and Sharpening Key Thinking Skills
Week 8	Read Research Articles: Howard & Jones (2000); Travis (2011); Oliver & Kowalczyk (2013) Reading Assignment: Chapter 3 Chapter Test: Chapter 1	Chapter 3: Building Academic Skills Library Visit
Week 9	Bring 4 research articles to class Chapter Test: Chapter 3	Chapter 4: Strengthening Soft Skills GROUP WORK: Reviewing Articles and Selecting Article for Presentation
Week 10	Exploring the Research in Summary Worksheet Due Chapter Test: Chapter 4	GROUP WORK: Focus on understanding research article Demonstrating Knowledge and Skills
Week 11	Reading Assignment: Chapter 7	Chapter 7: Staying on Track and Celebrating Success
Week 12	Power Point Slides Due	GROUP WORK: Creating a master presentation slides and focus on delivery
Week 13	**Research Presentations**	Presentations on Student Success Research
Week 14	Reflection Paper Due Chapter Test: Chapter 7	Chapter 7: Staying on Track and Celebrating Success

Grading Information

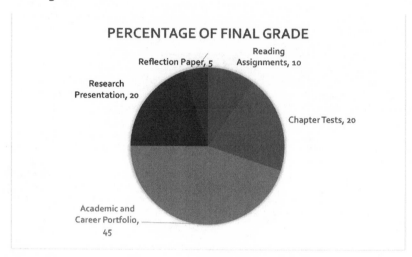

PERCENTAGE OF FINAL GRADE

Reflection Paper, 5 — Reading Assignments, 10

Research Presentation, 20

Chapter Tests, 20

Academic and Career Portfolio, 45

Final Letter Grade	Percentage at End of Semester
A	93-100
A-	90-92
B+	87-89
B	83-86
B-	80-82
C+	77-79
C	70-76
D	65-69
F	0-64

Assignment Details:

Reading Assignments (10%)

Students who engage in learning outside of the class are more likely to meet with success. Reading your textbook is one important way to familiarize yourself with course content, build active reading skills, and provide you with background knowledge needed for class activities. To help you get the most out of the reading experience, be sure to check out the Author videos in the e-book version. In addition, you'll need to respond to several reading questions for each chapter.

MindTap Chapter Tests (20%)

Successful students are engaged both in and out of the classroom. Because testing helps you learn, you will take an online test in Canvas on each chapter. *Please note that you will need the MindTap access code to take the tests.* You will be able to take two tests per chapter and the highest score will count.

Academic and Career Portfolio (45%)

Choosing a career path is a big decision that takes much time and effort. Engaging in the career exploration process will help you make a good decision. Even if you have already decided on a career path, this assignment will help you learn more about the various options that exist within the career of interest and will help you develop a plan of action. The final project will be an eight to 10-page paper (2-3 pages for each section below):

- Self-Assessment (10%): Knowing about yourself is an important part of the career exploration process. After discussing the self-assessment component of career decision-making and completing assessments, **summarize your values, abilities, personality, and interests**. You can do this via a brief paper, a visual document or website.

- Career Information Worksheets and Presentation (15%): Gather information from a variety of sources such as websites, informational interviews, and social media on at least three career paths. Complete the **Career Information Worksheets** on each career and write a personal reflection summary statement, addressing how the career paths are or are not aligned to your values, abilities, personality, and interests. You'll want to find out the following information on each career:
  - o Job description and job tasks
  - o Job outlook and salary
  - o Work environment and opportunities for advancement
  - o Education and other requirements
  - o Factors that contribute to success in this field
  - o Informational interview data or information gathered via social media
  - o Citation/source
  You will present the information you've researched to the class.

- Career Networking Actions and Reflection (10%): One of the most important skills to develop when it comes to careers is networking and it is never too soon to start networking. Complete the **Networking Action Plan** and then engage in at least three networking behaviors such as meeting with a professional in the field or attending a professional meeting and then write a summary of your experiences as well as a plan to continue developing your networking skills.

- Educational and Financial Plan (10%): Choose one of the career paths and develop an educational and financial plan. It will be helpful to meet with your advisor as you create your plans. The written plan should include:
  - o Statement about why the selected major works with your chosen career pathway.
  - o An Educational Map of courses you need to take and when you plan to take these courses. Indicate how each course counts (general education, major, elective) and identify outside of class activities you plan to take advantage of on the **Academic Plan.**
  - o Transition plan. If you are planning to transfer upon graduation, identify one or two colleges or universities you are considering transferring to after you graduate. Describe why you selected these colleges/universities and investigate the transferability of your degree program. If you are not planning to transfer, identify at least two potential entry-level positions in your field of interest and describe how college will help prepare you for these positions. Document your responses using the **Transition Plan.**

o   Financial plan. Determine the cost of your education. Explain how you plan to pay for college. If you are planning to take out a loan, use an online loan repayment calculator to determine how much you will need to pay monthly and how long it will take for you to pay off the loan. **Complete Financing Your Education Worksheet.**

Research Paper and Presentation Assignment (20%)

There are three graded components of the project: completing the Exploring the Research in Summary Worksheet, creating Power Point slides, and preparing a 10-15-minute group presentation. The same topic will be used for the worksheet and presentation. All members of your group will need to agree on an article and it needs to be approved by me. The purpose of this assignment is to help you build skills such as collaboration, communication, critical thinking, and information literacy skills that will serve you well in college and in your career. This project will consist of a combination of independent and collaborative work.

STEP 1- Choose the Article: Each group member should identify at least four peer-reviewed journal articles on a student success topic. Please note that all of the articles do not have to be on the same topic. You will share the articles with your group members and decide which research study to present on (needs to be approved by me).

STEP 2- Summarize the Article (Independently Graded, 5%): Complete the **Exploring the Research in Summary Worksheet for the selected peer-reviewed research article.** Note: all members of the group will be summarizing the same article but you need to work independently- not together for this part of the project.

STEP 3: Ensure All Member Understand the Study: Group members will discuss the study, making sure all group members understand the major points and findings of the selected article.

STEP 4: Creating a Power Point Presentation (Independently Graded, 5%): Each member needs to create visually effective and informative slides that summarize the study. Mayer's multi-media principles need to be used to create the slides.

STEP 5: Combine Slides to Create a Master Slide Presentation: After receiving feedback on this assignment, you will then all get together and create one master slide presentation, using the best components of previously designed slides or developing new ones as needed.

STEP 6: Focus on Delivery of Presentation: You will then shift your attention to the best way to deliver the content, using strategies to highlight important points during the presentation. Be sure to review and incorporate effective presentation strategies discussed in the text. Next, practice, practice, practice! All group members need to be able to present the entire presentation. View this as an independent project with a support team.

STEP 7: Present! (Grade- Your Performance 5%; Overall Presentation Quality 5%): *Note that you will be randomly assigned a part of the presentation to present on the day of the presentation.*

Reflection Paper (5%)

At the end of the semester, you will write a three to five page reflection paper that addresses the following questions:

- What did you learn about yourself via the assessments and the course? What are your strengths? What areas can you improve upon? How will this information be helpful to you as a student and in your career?
- How much progress have you made toward your academic and career goals? How has this course helped you develop and work toward your goals? What additional action steps can you take to make further progress and achieve your goals?

About the Authors

Christine Harrington is a national expert in student success and teaching and learning. Christine earned her BA in psychology and MA in counseling and personnel services from the College of New Jersey and her PhD in counseling psychology from Lehigh University. She has worked in higher education for almost twenty years. She began her career as a full-time counselor at Middlesex County College in Edison, New Jersey, where she provided academic, career, and personal counseling to a diverse student population. While serving in this role, Christine started teaching a first-year seminar course as well as psychology courses as an adjunct professor. After spending approximately seven years in student services, Christine shifted to a full-time position as professor of psychology and student success. In this role, she was also the first-year seminar course coordinator and the director for the Center for the Enrichment of Learning and Teaching. Christine has also been teaching part-time in the Learning and Teaching Department within the Graduate School of Education at Rutgers University. Most recently, she has a two-year appointment as the executive director for the Center for Student Success at the New Jersey Council of County Colleges. In this role, she assists all nineteen New Jersey community colleges in implementing Guided Pathways to improve student success outcomes. At the conclusion of her two-year term, she will return to the classroom, teaching student success and psychology again at Middlesex County College.

Christine is the author of a research-based first-year seminar textbook aligned to Guided Pathways, *Student Success in College: Doing What Works! 3rd edition.* She coauthored *Dynamic Lecturing: Research-Based Strategies to Enhance Lecture Effectiveness* (with Todd Zakrajsek) and *Designing a Motivational Syllabus: Creating a Learning Path for Student Engagement* (with Melissa Thomas). She is a contributing author of *Founda-*

tions for Critical Thinking, published by the National Resource Center for the First-Year Experience and Students in Transition. She was the 2016 recipient of the Excellence in Teaching First-Year Experience Award, which was presented at the Annual Conference on the First-Year Experience, and the recipient of the 2016 Middlesex County College Faculty Excellence in Teaching Award. She is frequently invited to give plenary presentations at national and local conferences as well as at colleges and universities across the nation.

Theresa Orosz earned her AAS degree in accounting from Middlesex County College, her BS in management science and MA in liberal studies from Kean University, and her EdD in educational leadership from Rowan University. She has worked in higher education for twenty-six years but began her career as an accountant for the federal government and in private industry before returning to her alma mater, Middlesex County College, as a business instructor in the continuing education division of the college. She went on to manage MCC's Career Services Office for thirteen years before joining the Academic Advising Center as assistant director. She worked for the vice president for academic and student affairs prior to assuming her current position as assistant dean of the Division of Arts and Sciences. She has ten years of adjunct experience as an instructor of the cooperative education seminar and the student success course.

Theresa has led or been a member of various campus committees in addition to being chairperson of the college's governance body. She is currently the leader of the institution's Guided Pathways team. Theresa is an advisory board member of the New Jersey Center for Student Success. She has previously held positions within in the New Jersey Cooperative Education and Internship Association, serving as vice president for finance, communications, and programs before becoming president. She has presented on a variety of topics at regional and national conferences and was a 2017 recipient of the New Jersey Council of County College's Community College Spirit Award.